WHO ARE YOU ANYWAY?

EXPLORING EXODUS 34:6-7

Russell Bloodworth, Jr.

In general, Biblical quotes are taken primarily from the Lockman Foundation's New American
Standard Bible® (NASB), Copyright © 1960, 1962, 1963, 1968, 1971, 1972, 1973, 1975, 1977, 1995
by The Lockman Foundation and used by permission. (www.Lockman.org).

The key English translation of Exodus 34:6-7 is taken from the New English Translation
of the Book of Exodus, Vol. 2, as published in 1997 and edited by Rabbi A.J. Rosenberg.
The transliteration of Hebrew words is generally taken from Strong's Hebrew Lexicon.
Unfortunately, there are several ways to spell any Hebrew word in English because English letters
are being used to approximate Hebrew pronunciation. Different sources use different ways.

Cover Painting by Artist Umberto Marigliani; private collection.

ISBN: 978-1-09837-789-2

*For all of my Grandchildren, both those present
(Tully, Jack, William, Claire, Christopher, Parker, Emmy,
Ellen, Jonathan, Teddy, Oliver) and those to come.
Pops loves you very much!*

Table of Contents

PREFACE

"God, may He be exalted, knows that I have never ceased to be exceedingly apprehensive about setting down those things that I wish to set down in this treatise.... However, I have relied on two premises, the one being (the sages') saying in a similar case, "It is time to do something for the Lord" (Ps. 119:126) ... the second being their saying, 'Let all your acts be for the sake of heaven' (Ethics of the Fathers 7:7)."

(Maimonides, Guide to the Perplexed, Part One).

Fifty-three years ago, as a Thord-Gray Scholar in Sweden, I was exploring answers to several sets of questions. The questions were focused on ways that we can make our cities better by reforming the pattern of our expanding suburbs. But there were additional questions on my mind in 1968.

I was living with a Swedish family in the newly minted suburb of Stockholm—the village of Vallingby—a "new town" in the terminology of Socialist Sweden. My scholarship was structured around "independent study." In other words, the scholarship allowed me to set my own schedule and my own course of study. Having a bit of expense-paid freedom, I could structure every day as I wished.

After being solidly focused on architecture for five long years of under-graduate toil, I felt this Scandinavian sojourn offered me a chance to do some "catch-up." There were numerous subjects the architecture program at the University of Virginia forced me to skip. Socialism/Communism, World History, and World Religions were three missing building blocks. I was twenty-two years of age and felt a deep need to be more certain of my beliefs and direction for the future.

A solution seemed evident: rigidly divide each day into study blocks of 90 minutes. While I would devote three hours a day to investigations into architecture and city planning, I could devote 90-minute blocks for the study of World History, World Religions, Socialism and Communism.

I wanted to read from the original sources and dove into the Bhagavad Gita and other Hindu texts, Taoist teachings, Buddhism, Confucianism and general Muslim Doctrine. There was plenty to consider.

As my time in Sweden came to an end, I happened upon an English book shop in downtown Stockholm. It was late in the afternoon. Evenings during wintertime came early, and the shop lights were brightly shining. Scanning a table of featured paperbacks, I spied a very thin English New Testament. Compared to the books I had been reading, it seemed thin indeed. To finish off my academic schedule, I bought the little book with the intention of reading it over the next week.

Vallingby is about a 40-minute Tunnelbana (tunnel rail) ride from the center of Stockholm. Well-lit, the Tunnelbana allowed me to begin reading a few minutes after leaving the book shop. As the train car rolled along the tracks, I continued to read. I was well hooked by the time I arrived in

Vallingby and continued to read through the night until I finished around 5 a.m. What a read and what an impact!

Having read the other religious treatises over the course of many months, I was overwhelmed with the sense of truth and reality that I found in the New Testament. I had been worrying with the "God" question for some time, but now I felt compelled to make a serious course change. I returned to the States a committed Christian.

I was a committed Christian but still fuzzy on Who this God was with Whom I had begun a lifelong relationship. A book that was helpful to me at this point was by an American theologian living in Switzerland: *"He Is There and He Is Not Silent."* Francis Schaeffer's title to the book and accompanying content answered my most fundamental question. Yes, *"He is there and He is not silent!"*

My journey in God and toward God was accelerating. At the prompting of my college friend, Lewis Nix, I headed to Yale University in 1971 for graduate studies in environmental design. That allowed me to take advantage of a course being offered by Abraham Malherbe, the Buckingham Professor of New Testament Criticism and Interpretation at Yale's Divinity School. Browsing through the Divinity School's bookstore one brisk fall afternoon, I came across a small paperback treatise on distinctive ideas in Hebrew Scriptures by Norman Snaith. A compelling read, Snaith explored ancient Hebrew terms that were distinctive from the Semitic languages of the Middle East.

Short enough to be read in one afternoon but packed full of research on unique concepts, I read it that very day. One topic in particular caught my attention—the idea of covenant and the related Hebrew words: *BERIYTH (BRIT)* and *CHESED (HESED)*. I am sorry to say that it would be nearly fifteen years before I began to connect those Hebrew words with Moses's momentous mountaintop experience with God on Mount Sinai.

This book is an effort to convey what I have been trying to grasp for fifty years—all summed up in two succinct verses of the 34th Chapter of Exodus. I needed to write this book for myself if no one else. New vistas open for each of us as we consider afresh even the smallest insight. The Psalmist was correct; *"His Word is a lamp unto our feet."* (Psalm 119:105).

SPECIAL THANKS

I owe a huge debt of thanks to a great many people, but six must be mentioned. First, my wife, Fran Bloodworth, who has put up with a year of my research, strewn papers, and editorial questions. Then, my daughter Elizabeth Bloodworth Mitchell and my son Christopher Bloodworth have been absolute saints, using their remarkable textual skills without a moment's complaint to uncover numerous issues that had to be addressed. Fourth, my friend and longtime mentor, Terry Sanford Smith, who has been a constant cheerleader in what has ended up being a much longer process than anticipated.

Finally, my friends Norma and Martin Sarvis, longtime residents of Israel ministering through *Kav Kavod* (Line of Glory) and *Succat Hallel* (Tent of Praise), have been a true blessing. Overflowing with encouragement, Martin patiently helped me overcome numerous Hebrew language stumbling blocks. Without question, this book would never been printed without his immense insight into the Hebrew Scriptures.

A WORD FOR THE JOURNEY

I will be calling the LORD of the Universe by masculine pronouns throughout. But let me be clear: that is simply my convention. I primarily relate to the Creator as Father, while the LORD relates to me as both Father *and* Mother. For example, *"Can a woman forget her nursing child, or show no compassion for the child of her womb? Even these may forget, yet I will not forget you."* (Isaiah 49:15). Or God speaking of the exiled tribe of Ephraim as *His* child, *"'...Therefore my heart ["womb"] yearns for him. I will surely have compassion upon him,' says the LORD."* (Jeremiah 31:20).

Regardless, God's relationship with us is parental, familial. Man and woman were both made in His image. I think I can safely say that the LORD of the Universe is beyond gender. Clement of Alexandria, writing in the 37th chapter of his *Paedagogus* around 198 C.E. reflected, *"In His ineffable essence He is father; in His compassion to us He became mother."* In fact, one of the special attributes revealed in God's declaration to Moses is decidedly feminine in nature. This is particularly true of the word we translate as compassion. An associated word in Hebrew is the word for womb.

For proper names in Scripture, I have generally used standard English forms rather than transcriptions of the Hebrew. Thus, Moses and not Moshe, Jacob and not Ya'akov. In transcribing Hebrew words, you will find rough English equivalents rather than a "scientific" transcription. I am amazed how varied Hebrew words can be written in English. For example, *chesed, chessed, hesed,* and *khesed* are four ways of spelling in English letters the Hebrew word for loving-kindness.

Regarding the English word *loving-kindness*: for consistency's sake, I have taken the liberty of rendering the word with a hyphen throughout—even when quoting directly from the New American Standard translation.

CHAPTER ONE

The Most Important Question

"Who are you anyway?" An important question, but even more important is the same question posed to the Creator of the Universe. That is the most important question because until you can answer that question, the second most important question for any person cannot be adequately framed—the question, "Who am *I* anyway?"

Every generation, no matter the geographic location, has grappled with both questions and the possible answers. Today, in developed countries around the world, few struggle with the question about a Creator; they push the question away, far from consciousness. Yet, individuals still are faced with the second question, and it is harder to push away: the question—"Who am I?"

Only with the first question answered can we focus on the second since the very image of the Creator is revealed in all us. If you don't know Who God is, you really can't know fully who you are. This is doubly true for both

Jews and Christians because each group believes that Genesis 1:27 is true: *"So God created man in His own image; in the image of God He created him; male and female He created them."*

Over the millennia, many have tried to answer the question, "God, Who are You anyway?" The wonderful thing is that God has answered this question to a great degree in our Bibles, both the Bible of our Jewish friends as well as the Bible of our Christian friends. In one sense, both Bibles present the same answer.

What is this Creator God truly like? Is He like the God of the movies (think Cecil B. DeMille's *The Ten Commandments*)? What is His character? Is He an angry God (think of Jonathan Edwards's famous sermon, *Sinners in the Hands of an Angry God*)? Is He remote and far away, or is He closer than the blood in your veins? Who is He anyway?

Jews and Christians will undoubtedly offer different responses to this important question. My Jewish friends will emphasize God's Oneness and His Otherness. The Almighty is beyond comprehension and even His infinite nature cannot be probed. Yet they will affirm that we are made in His image and that He has spoken to and through His Prophets about His ways.

Christians may offer a different response, "Well, Jesus is God, so God is just like Jesus." What they mean is that Jesus demonstrated what God was like because they believe Jesus to be both fully man and fully God. So, when you see Jesus, you see God. If you want to know Who God is, just look at Jesus.

"'If you really know me, you will know my Father as well. From now on, you do know him and have seen him.' Philip said, 'LORD, show us the Father and that will be enough for us.' Jesus answered: 'Don't you know me, Philip, even

after I have been among you such a long time? Anyone who has seen me has seen the Father. How can you say, 'Show us the Father?'" (The Gospel of John, Chapter 14:7-9).

Given their belief, it makes sense for Christians to take this view. However, one practical challenge with this way of knowing God is that one must grasp all that Jesus both said and did to really draw any conclusions. To do that, we have to take Jesus's rich and complex life history recorded in Scripture and integrate it into a functional understanding of what Jesus's life means with regard to his character. From Jesus's character, we can deduce God's character.

But that is a lot easier said than done. From my experience, it takes a very long time to develop a mature understanding of just Who this God is—the God that the theologian Francis Schaeffer declares, *"is there and is not silent"*—through the study of Scripture.

Some Christians will jump in at this point and remind us that Jesus promised that the Spirit of God would come after his resurrection and that God's Spirit, *"... will receive from me [Jesus] what he will make known to you.... Very truly I tell you, my Father will give you whatever you ask in my name. Until now you have not asked for anything in my name. Ask and you will receive, and your joy will be complete."* (John 16:15, 23-24).

"And I will do whatever you ask in my name, so that the Father may be glorified in the Son. You may ask me for anything in my name, and I will do it." (John 14:13-14).

Fellow Christians are assured that the Father of the Universe will make known to them what they ask in the name of Jesus. He will make known Who He is in His very nature if we ask Him.

"Whoever has my commands and keeps them is the one who loves me. The one who loves me will be loved by my Father, and I too will love them and show myself to them." (John 14:21).

At this point, if you are a Christian, it would be reasonable for you to ask, "If these promises are true, is there any reason to be reading this book?" I would say "yes" from the simple hope that unpacking some key foundational Hebrew Scriptures might be worthwhile—helping you more quickly grasp the character of God—His ways and what motivates Him.

Plus, the greatest safeguard in our individual journey is Holy Scripture. I have been married to my wife, Fran, for a long time. For our 47th anniversary, I gave her a card whose cover featured a simple message: *"Adventures Guaranteed; Instructions NOT Included!"* Inside, I wrote how thankful I was that instructions WERE included when we got married.

We both had our Bibles. They were filled with marriage instructions, and we took those instructions seriously from the beginning. Honestly, without those instructions, I doubt we would have been married 47 years. We need every trustworthy instruction we can get, and where better than the Bible!

I believe the same is true regarding answering the question of, "God, Who are You anyway?" Scriptural boundaries are a great safeguard!

CHAPTER TWO

On the Mountaintop

EXODUS 34:6-7

"And the LORD passed before him and proclaimed, יְהֹוָה יְהֹוָה, God, Who is compassionate and gracious, slow to anger and abundant in loving-kindness and truth; preserving loving-kindness for thousands, forgiving iniquity, rebellion and sin; yet He does not completely clear [of sin]. He visits the iniquity of parents on the children and children's children, to the third and fourth generations."[1]

Two of the most important verses in the entire Bible are Exodus 34:6-7. These verses come in the midst of the retelling of one of the most exciting, challenging and dramatic events of all time. The context in which the LORD spoke this revelation is important.

---

1 From the Modern English Translation of the Complete *Tanakh* (Tanach), The Book of Exodus, Vol. 2, as edited by Rabbi A.J. Rosenberg.

The great Israeli Exodus occurred over 3,000 years ago. The God of Abraham, Isaac and Israel (Jacob) had mightily delivered their descendants from Egypt after difficult but miraculous negotiations with Pharaoh. Three months after crossing the Red Sea, Moses along with the Israelites, *"came to the wilderness of Sinai...camped in front of the mountain."* (Exodus 19:2).

There, Moses has multiple encounters with the God Who had so powerfully delivered them from Egypt. After encamping, Moses goes up onto Mount Sinai and hears God speaking to him.

God offers those at the foot of the mountain a unique arrangement: *"... if you will indeed obey My voice and keep My covenant, then you shall be My own possession among all the peoples, for all the earth is Mine; and you shall be to Me a kingdom of priests and a holy nation."* Moses descends, calls the leaders of the people, and shares God's offer. Perhaps we shouldn't be surprised, but the people accept, replying, *"All that the LORD has spoken we will do!"* (Exodus 19:5-8).

At God's direction, the Israelites consecrate themselves and wash their clothes to be ready for a more intimate encounter with this great God.

"So it came about on the third day, when it was morning, that there were thunder and lightning flashes and a thick cloud upon the mountain and a very loud trumpet sound, so that all the people who were in the camp trembled...and they stood at the foot of the mountain.

The traditional Mount Sinai taken c. 1870 by Elijah Walton

"Now Mount Sinai was all in smoke because the LORD descended upon it in fire; and its smoke ascended like the smoke of a furnace, and the whole mountain quaked violently. When the sound of the trumpet grew louder and louder, Moses spoke, and God answered him with thunder. The LORD came down on Mount Sinai, to the top of the mountain; and the LORD called Moses to the top of the mountain, and Moses went up." (Exodus 19:16-20).

THE TEN COMMANDMENTS

The LORD then declares what the whole world has come to know as the *Ten Commandments:*

"You shall have no other gods before Me.

"You shall not make for yourself an idol, or any likeness of what is in heaven above or on the earth beneath, or in the water under the earth. You shall not worship them nor serve them....

"You shall not take the name of the LORD your God in vain, for the LORD will not leave him unpunished who takes His name in vain.

"Remember the Sabbath day, to keep it holy. For six days you shall labor and do all your work, but the seventh day is a Sabbath of the LORD your God; on it you shall not do any work, you, or your son, or your daughter, your male slave or your female slave, or your cattle, or your resident who stays with you. For in six days the LORD made the heavens and the earth, the sea and everything that is in them, and He rested on the seventh day; for that reason the LORD blessed the Sabbath day and made it holy.

"Honor your father and your mother, that your days may be prolonged in the land which the LORD your God gives you.

"You shall not murder.

"You shall not commit adultery.

"You shall not steal.

"You shall not bear false witness against your neighbor.

"You shall not covet your neighbor's house; you shall not covet your neighbor's wife or his male servant or his female servant or his ox or his donkey or any-thing that belongs to your neighbor." (Exodus 20:3-17).

Quaking, flames, smoke, lightning and thunder covered the great mountain. The people said YES to this great LORD—they would obey! During a three-month period, Moses ascends and descends Mt. Sinai at least five times as he draws near to God's presence. In the midst of this ascending and descending, the LORD inscribes on tablets of stone the Ten Commandments. Down below, Moses's fellow travelers simultaneously commit an unthinkable iniquity. Fearing that Moses has died during his last ascent, they do the very thing they had promised not to do—they form a golden calf to worship and follow:

"Now when the people saw that Moses delayed to come down from the mountain, the people assembled about Aaron and said to him, 'Come, make us a god who will go before us; as for this Moses, the man who brought us up from the land of Egypt, we do not know what has become of him.'" (Exodus 32:1).

TROUBLE BELOW

Aaron, Moses's brother, does exactly what the people want. Meanwhile, up on the mountain, God alerts Moses of the rank revelry and rebellion breaking out in the camp below:

"Your people...have corrupted themselves. They have quickly turned aside from the way which I commanded them. They have made for themselves a molten calf and have worshiped it and have sacrificed to it and said, 'This is your god, O Israel, Who brought you up from the land of Egypt!'" (Exodus 32:7-8).

God's response is anger, intensified no doubt by memory of the covenants He had made with Abraham, Isaac and Israel (*Jacob*) many centuries earlier. Israel's descendants had verbally affirmed from their side a more extensive covenant only a few days before. Now, they were blatantly disobeying the first two commandments they had agreed to follow. Moses, no doubt terrified and dumbfounded by the events taking place, entreats God to remember His special relationship with the three deceased Patriarchs. Moses pleads,

"Remember Abraham, Isaac, and Israel, Your servants to whom You swore by Yourself, and said to them, 'I will multiply your descendants as the stars of the heavens, and all this land of which I have spoken I will give to your

descendants, and they shall inherit it forever.' So, the LORD changed His mind about the harm which He said He would do to His people." (Exodus 32:13-14).

In delving into God's nature, there is a good bit we could explore here, but my main intention is to set the scene for what happens in Chapter 34.

Moses descends the mountain with the two stone tablets inscribed by God with Ten Commandments, the first two of which the Israelites had just directly disobeyed: "You shall have no other gods before Me. You shall not make for yourself an idol, or any likeness of what is in heaven above or on the earth beneath or in the water under the earth. You shall not worship them or serve them...." (Exodus 20:3-5).

Unfortunately,

"It came about, as soon as Moses came near the camp, that he saw the calf and the dancing; and Moses's anger burned, and he threw the tablets from his hands and shattered them at the foot of the mountain. He took the calf which they had made and burned it with fire, and ground it to powder, and scattered it over the surface of the water and made the sons of Israel drink it." (Exodus 32:19-20).

And that was not the end of it. The Levites who rallied to the LORD were sent throughout the camp to kill any who had participated in the iniquity. The language may imply those punished were Levites as well. What is certain is that Moses goes back up the mountain the next morning to plead forgiveness for the people and make a remarkable request in case forgiveness was not granted. Moses undoubtedly was turned upside down inside.

"Then Moses returned to the LORD, and said, 'Alas, this people has committed a great sin, and they have made a god of gold for themselves. But now, *if You will, forgive their sin—and if not, please blot me out from Your book which You have written!"* (Exodus 32:31-32).

This was a remarkable appeal and a selfless one. The drama does not diminish.

"The LORD said to Moses, 'Whoever has sinned against Me, I will blot him out of My book. But go now, lead the people where I told you.'" (Exodus 32:33-34).

"'Go up to a land flowing with milk and honey; for I will not go up in your midst, because you are an obstinate people, and I might destroy you on the way.' When the people heard this sad word, they went into mourning....." (Exodus 33:3-4).

This prepares us for what happens next. It is a bit hard to get into Moses's head at this point because so much has happened. He has perhaps a million Israelites out in the middle of the Sinai Peninsula. Previously, Moses and the Israelites had some degree of confidence that they might survive the wilderness given the great miracles that they had seen this God perform. But if the LORD's presence did not go with them, who knew what would happen? Plus, Moses, raised as an Egyptian, carried a mantle of suspicion amongst the people. To make matters worse, this great God Who had identified Himself initially in a burning bush was unbelievably powerful. Moses had seen that over and over—most recently by his experience on the mountain.

Considering his state, it is not surprising that Moses chooses to request two favors of the LORD:

"You say to me, 'Bring up this people!' But You Yourself have not let me know whom You will send with me. Moreover, You have said, 'I have known you by name, and you have also found favor in My sight.' Now therefore, I pray You,

*if I have found favor in Your sight, **let me know Your ways** that I may know You, so that I may find favor in Your sight. Consider too, that this nation is Your people."* (Exodus 33:12-13).

Amazingly, God grants both requests in response to Moses's plea. As to who will go with Moses and the Israelites, it will be God Himself—His Presence *will* go with them. Second, as for showing Moses His ways, that is, the nature of God's essence, the LORD Himself will answer Moses. First, The LORD has Moses place himself in a cleft of the mountain so that the LORD's presence might "pass by" and His "ways" be proclaimed.

This "passing by" scene is beyond me—beyond my ability to fully conceive or imagine. It is hard to put our feet into Moses's sandals!

In the cleft of the rock, Moses is shielded from the most powerful Being imaginable by the Creator's "hand," (picture an incredible cloud, burning energy, something beyond all understanding). Moses hears the Almighty proclaim His *"ways"* and later records these words in Hebrew (which there-fore must be read from right to left):

וַיַּעֲבֹ֨ר יְהוָ֥ה ׀ עַל־פָּנָיו֮ וַיִּקְרָא֒

יְהוָ֣ה ׀ יְהוָ֔ה אֵ֥ל רַח֖וּם וְחַנּ֑וּן אֶ֥רֶךְ אַפַּ֖יִם וְרַב־חֶ֥סֶד וֶאֱמֶֽת׃

נֹצֵ֥ר חֶ֙סֶד֙ לָאֲלָפִ֔ים נֹשֵׂ֥א עָוֺ֛ן וָפֶ֖שַׁע וְחַטָּאָ֑ה וְנַקֵּה֙ לֹ֣א יְנַקֶּ֔ה

פֹּקֵ֣ד ׀ עֲוֺ֣ן אָב֗וֹת עַל־בָּנִים֙ וְעַל־בְּנֵ֣י בָנִ֔ים עַל־שִׁלֵּשִׁ֖ים וְעַל־

רִבֵּעִֽים׃

If we translate the Hebrew text into English characters to be read out loud, we get a rough proximation of the sounds (reading left to right):

Va-ya'avor YHVH al-panav va-yikra

YHVH, YHVH el rachuwm v'channuwn erekh apayim v'rav chesed v'emeth. Notser chesed la'alaphim nosei a-von va-pesha v'chatta'ah v'naqei lo y'naqei poqed avon avot al-banim v'al-banei vanim al-shilleshim v'al-ribe'im.

And finally, following the Modern English Translation edited by Rabbi Rosenberg:

"And the LORD passed before him and proclaimed, יְהֹוָה יְהֹוָה, God, Who is compassionate and gracious, slow to anger and abundant in loving-kindness and truth; preserving loving-kindness for thousands, forgiving iniquity, rebellion and sin; yet He does not completely clear [of sin]. He visits the iniquity of parents on the children and children's children, to the third and fourth generations." (Exodus 34:6-7).

We will unpack the key Hebrew words as best we can, but before we do, let's step back and think about their importance. These two verses, partially or in full, are repeated more than any other two verses in the Bible. Many theologians call them the Credo of the Hebrew Scriptures, that is, the core revelation of just Who God is.

THE THIRTEEN ATTRIBUTES OF MERCY

In rabbinic tradition, these two verses contain the "Thirteen Attributes of Mercy" *(Shelosh-Esreh Middot HaRakhamim)* that describe God and His ways, though different Jewish streams focus on different words in the two verses. Generally, they are recited on Jewish "Holy Days" when the *Sefer Torah* (the Book of the Commandments) is taken from the Ark in the synagogue. In some synagogues, the Thirteen Attributes are recited by the entire congregation while the congregation is fasting. The attributes are closely tied to the covenant God made with Israel on the mountain.

CONTEXT

Context is important. When someone asks us a question, our answer is colored by the context of the question. Moses asks the God of the Universe to describe His ways immediately after the horrific Golden Calf episode. A terrible iniquity has occurred. "What, God, are you going to do with us?" "What kind of God are You anyway?" "Will we be safe, or will You destroy us before we come to the end of our journey?" What will this powerful God say about His ways in light of the disaster?

God's declaration is bracketed by human failure in the Israelite camp on one hand and God's intention to renew the covenant on the other. Immediately after the revelation of His ways, we come to verse 10 where, in spite of the Golden Calf debacle, God shows His intention to renew the covenant made only a few weeks earlier:

"Then God said, 'Behold, I am going to make a covenant....'" (Exodus 34:10).

Human frailty on one side and God's covenantal intentions on the other affect the words God chooses to speak. When you look closely at what is said, you can see that God appears to be addressing Israel's overt rebellion directly. But instead of stressing how He may hold the rebellious accountable, God stresses His immense compassion, graciousness, patience and relational faithfulness. His choice of words must have come as a big surprise—welcome news to both Moses and the people who heard Moses repeat the words.

In Exodus 34:6-7, our Creator reveals characteristics that you likely would not associate with a God Who had days before revealed Himself in fire and thunder—a Creator God Who does astounding, terrifying miracles—a God Who, as C.S. Lewis wrote, *"is not safe.... But,"* as Lewis continued,

"He's good!"[2] God reveals His wonderful relational ways to Moses: compassionate, gracious, reliable, lovingly steadfast, totally truthful, slow to anger, and remarkably forgiving, but not so forgiving that His forgiveness cancels the positive side of the consequences of bad actions or attitudes.

Another side of this coin is what God did NOT say. There is no mention of many attributes that surely must be ascribed to God: attributes like eternal, holy, powerful, invisible and so forth. This is not because God is not these things. I think it is because God wanted Moses to understand what undergirded His actions—what propelled His "ways"—at that crucial point in Moses's life history.

GOOD NEWS

What we see revealed is God's HEART. His innermost core is being revealed—what propels His actions.

Recognizing that God's declaration is specific to a moment in time does not change the fact that this "news" of God's "ways" is very good news indeed. In fact, we could call it "gospel," that is, mighty good news! This good news flows directly out of God's character, that is, Who He is.

An incident with my father comes to mind. Perhaps twelve or thirteen years old at the time, I was at an age when parents are ready to ship their children off to reform school. I came home from school in a lousy mood, said something I shouldn't have, and I can remember my mother distinctly saying, "Your father will deal with you when he comes home!" Dad was a very hardworking sales manager who was responsible for over eighty salesmen. Tired after a demanding day at work, Dad drove up our driveway while I trembled inside. Mother briefed him, and off he and I went to the small attic that extended beyond my upstairs bedroom.

2 C.S. Lewis. *The Lion, the Witch and The Wardrobe,* Chapter Eight.

I knew I deserved what was coming. Dad sat me down on a stool and proceeded to take off his belt (standard parental practice during the 1950s). My heart sank, but Dad gave me a little wink of kindness as he struck the floor instead of me—all for Mother's consumption. I suppose Moses also was expecting a different outcome until he heard God's proclamation. Like my Dad, God is filled with great compassion and graciousness. He is slow to anger and abounding in loving-kindness.

God's proclamation can be organized from a "good news" standpoint. There is the portion that precedes the declaration *"And the LORD passed before him and proclaimed...."* Then we have the section of clearly positive characteristics: *"YHVH, YHVH, God, compassionate and gracious, slow to anger, and abundant in loving-kindness and truth; preserving loving-kindness for thousands, forgiving iniquity, rebellion and sin...."* Finally, we end with what appears to be the tougher section: *"yet He does not completely clear [of sin]. He visits the iniquity of parents on the children and the children's children to the third and fourth generations."* Many scholars view the third part as "bad" news, but I don't think that is necessarily so. We will explore that issue when we get to Chapter Eleven.

TRANSLATION DIFFICULTY

Unfortunately, many of our English translations fall short—in some cases, very short—in translating the meaning of the most important Hebrew words in Exodus 34:6-7. For one thing, it is amazingly difficult to translate any ancient language that differs significantly from your own. The culture is different, the words are different, and sometimes the alphabet is different as well. Plus, the order of words as well as the grammar can differ. And, unlike English, ancient Hebrew uses few "helping" words. Punctuation and vowel sounds in ancient Hebrew texts are non-existent. Add over 3,000 years of time passage and an "accurate" translation is difficult to accomplish! We would need divine help!

A good example of the translation challenge in the words Moses records is the Hebrew word **CHESED**. **CHESED** shows up twice in Exodus 34:6-7. The word does not have an exact English parallel. The word meaning for **CHESED** involves strong love, steadfast faithfulness, and is closely associated with the glue that holds together a binding covenant.

Some translators use the words "Loyal Love" to get closer to the meaning of **CHESED**. But instead of loyal love or steadfast love, many of our English translations translate the word as "mercy." This might have made sense if one was translating from the Greek Septuagint instead of the original Hebrew, where the original translators of the Hebrew Scriptures into Greek used the Greek word ἔλεος for **CHESED**. The word ἔλεος is illustrated in English characters as *eleos*. *Eleos* simply means "mercy." In my view, this is a long way from an accurate rendition of the word **CHESED** in English. This will be clearer as we dive deeper into that word's meaning in Chapter Seven.

The Jubilee Bible translation illustrates an example of the problem:

"And as the LORD passed by before him, He proclaimed, 'I AM, I AM strong, **merciful***, and gracious, longsuffering, and abundant in* **mercy** *and truth....'"*

Here, two very different Hebrew words from Exodus 34:6, **CHANNUWN** and **CHESED**, are translated respectively *"merciful"* and *"mercy,"* and the underlying word translated *"mercy"* is **CHESED**. We run into this confusion frequently in translations of **CHESED** in our English Bibles, particularly in the Psalms where the word "mercy" is used in place of something closer to the meaning of **CHESED**. It usually takes multiple English words to convey the true meaning—words like *loving-kindness, steadfast love,* and *loyal love.*

THE FLAME IN YOUR HAND

Since we are exploring Who God is, we want to get as close to the truth as possible. Before we take a deep dive in the chapters that follow, a final word of encouragement from Barbara Bowe's book, **Biblical Foundations of Spirituality**:

"When you hold a sacred text in your hands and ponder its wisdom, it is not enough to learn the meaning of the words alone. A sacred text is like the flame of a candle. You can observe its color and height; you can describe its many properties. You can smell its fragrance; watch the way the flame constantly flickers in the air. You can measure the intensity of its heat and light, and calculate how rapidly the candle will burn. But that is not yet enough to know it. It is not until you have touched your finger to the flame that you can know the real meaning of the candle. That is how it is with sacred texts."

By necessity, we will look at many word meanings during our journey. Don't allow those to get you sidetracked or cause you to miss the flame. This is the Creator and LORD of the Universe we are talking about! Pray that your heart as well as your mind will be open to His words! Touch the flame!

CHAPTER THREE

THE NAME

Our mission is to throw as much light as possible onto the Creator's personal revelation to Moses. Aside from the very act of coming to Moses and the children of Israel (from which we learn a great deal about Who God is and who we are), let's listen carefully to God's declaration and look at each individual word or phrase. Open your mind and your heart to these special words.

Overfamiliarity with English words often clouds our understanding; they rarely force their way into our minds and hearts where we can be hit with their deep meaning. It makes perfect sense that the Prophet Jeremiah uses the Hebrew term **KATHAB** (meaning "graven") when describing what God *wants* to do in our hearts. (Jeremiah 31:33). Let this be our goal: to let the God of the Universe engrave deeply in our hearts the wonder of each attribute.

Let me make a confession before we delve into the very first words where the Name of God is proclaimed: It is a challenge to approach this chapter. Many of my Jewish brothers and sisters approach even talking about God's Name as a Holy undertaking—one to be undertaken with the greatest of respect. I completely concur.

QODESH

An important help to our endeavor is the concept of **QODESH** *(KODESH)*— *something "set apart."* This word is most often translated in our Bibles as "holy." God Himself is **QODESH**. Two of the best English understandings of **QODESH** could be "a thing entirely set apart" or "belonging to the Other."

Our Creator is set entirely apart from all created things and all created beings. He is in a set by Himself. His OTHERNESS simply *is*. We see this **QODESH** reality in several Hebrew Scriptures. Perhaps the most illustrative (and frightening) is the story of King David, the Ark of the Covenant, and Uzzah as recounted in 1st Chronicles 13.

The Ark of the Covenant was devoted entirely to God. That fact made it **QODESH**, that is, belonging to the Otherness of God. David had two men assigned to drive the Ark on a cart. Ussah was one of those men. The oxen stumbled, the cart began to rock, and Uzzah stretched forth his hand to hold steady the teetering Ark. Immediately Uzzah died. David interpreted this event as the *"LORD God breaking out."* (1st Chronicles 15:13).

If ever there was anything "set apart" and entirely devoted to God, it was the Ark. It was **QODESH**, belonging entirely to God, and only the **QODESH** (those Levites who had gone through the priest-making process and been rendered devoted to God) could actually deal with it. It was entirely "set apart!" It seems clear that Uzzah was *not* a priest. David was careful not to make this mistake again. (See 1st Chronicles 15:2).

The story of Uzzah and the Ark underscores how even a priest in that era would have been extremely cautious dealing with any item devoted to the LORD. Now we must ask, "What could be more devoted to God than His very name?"

THE MEMORIAL NAME

You may know that there are four Hebrew letter characters that most Jewish people feel very hesitant to say aloud. Called the Tetragrammaton in Greek [*tetra* (four) + *gramma* (letter)], those four letters spell the name that the LORD many months earlier had called Himself when Moses had his "God encounter" at the Burning Bush in the wilderness. The four characters in English sound like "Yod-Heh-Vav-Heh" and are often written as YHVH because the sound of each character is reminiscent of a specific letter in the English alphabet. Let's look quickly at that passage in Exodus 3:15:

"God [ELOHIYM], furthermore, said to Moses, 'Thus you shall say to the sons of Israel, "The LORD [יְהֹוָה], the God [ELOHIYM] of your fathers, the God [ELOHIYM] of Abraham, the God [ELOHIYM] of Isaac, and the God [ELOHIYM] of Jacob, has sent me to you." THIS IS MY NAME FOREVER, AND THIS IS MY MEMORIAL-NAME TO ALL GENERATIONS.'" (Emphases mine).

Note the English word **LORD** in the preceding verse. It identifies the Hebrew word composed of the four Hebrew characters: יְהֹוָה. Over time, Jewish scholars, conscious of the sanctity of God's name, hesitated to say this word aloud. I get that; it is **QODESH**—belonging entirely to God—His Memorial Name. For this reason, other words were substituted in some Hebrew scrolls to actually *prevent* verbal articulation.

The Hebrew word **ADONAI** meaning "Lord" often replaced it. For example, in the **Shema**, the centerpiece of daily morning and evening Jewish prayer services, the word **ADONAI** is substituted for the underlying Hebrew "Memorial Name." Another "substitute" word is **HASHEM**, which simply means "The Name."

In contemporary translations, the *Complete Jewish Bible* uses **ADONAI** for the Memorial Name, while *The Israel Bible* and the *Orthodox Jewish Bible* use **HASHEM** as their replacement word. The revised *New American Standard Bible* (NASB) and the JPS *Tanakh* (1917) translations follow a more common convention of simply writing the English word LORD entirely in uppercase when God's Memorial Name is encountered. If you are using those translations, whenever you see the LORD fully capitalized, be aware that the underlying Hebrew word is likely God's Memorial Name.

Regarding the pronunciation of יְהֹוָה, there are many opinions but no certainty. It is difficult to be certain of the exact pronunciation for a variety of reasons, not the least of which is that Masoretic scribes of the Middle Ages were hesitant to make the pronunciation known by including vowel signs. That isn't a problem if one simply pronounces a substitute word—**ADONAI, HASHEM** or **LORD**.

It is easy to be confused with other Hebrew words designating God when reading almost any English translation. Two other Hebrew words employed in Genesis and Exodus frequently reference the Creator. One is the root word for a Deity: the Hebrew word **EL**, which is usually translated "God" in English. In ancient Semitic usage, the term references strength and power. It can refer to the chief deity, the creator god, and in some cases the god of a specific place or attribute. For the Israelites, **EL** became one of their names for God. It often appears with descriptors such as the word **SHADDAI**, which means "Almighty." **EL SHADDAI** will normally be translated "*God Almighty*" in English.

A more frequent reference for God in Scriptures is the word *ELOHIYM*—the plural of *EL*. *ELOHIYM* is used with much greater frequency in the Hebrew Scriptures as it can reference both the God of Abraham, foreign "gods," angels, and even judges. It can be translated in various ways depending on the context.

Rabbi Sforno (Obadiah ben Jacob Sforno), an important Italian rabbi of the sixteenth century, thought that, *"The reason that the term ... appears in the plural mode, 'ELOHIYM,' is to teach us that God is the origin of all the various visible and invisible manifestations in the universe."* *ELOHIYM* can be the God of the air and the God of the sea, the God of all compassion, as well as other things. Christians, on the other hand, see in the term a hint of the Trinity, that is, three "persons" in One. It is interesting to note, however, that when referencing the God of the Universe, *ELOHIYM* is used with a *singular* verb.

Certain translation conventions generally will be a signal of what the underlying Hebrew text is referencing. If you see "God Almighty," many translators are translating the words *EL SHADDAI*. If you see only the word "God," that usually means the underlying word is *ELOHIYM* even though sometimes the underlying word will be simply *EL*. And, of course, we know now that if you see the word LORD in caps, we have the underlying Memorial Name of God.

At first glance, it would appear that God's Memorial Name was known to multiple generations who descended from Abraham before God's encounters with Moses. Multiple verses in the Book of Genesis indicate that Abraham knew God by His Memorial Name and even declared it to the King of Sodom. (See Genesis 15:2 and 14:22). The same is true of Abraham's servant who appears to have known the LORD's Memorial Name and declared it to Laban, Rebekah's brother (when the servant was sent in search for a wife for Isaac, Abraham's son). The same is reflected in the texts of Genesis where Isaac prayed directly to the LORD, and again it appears that the LORD revealed His Memorial Name to Isaac's son, Jacob (later Israel), in the dream of the ladder set between Heaven and Earth. [3] But what throws that view into question is God's clarification to Moses as recorded in the book of Exodus:

*"God spoke further to Moses and said to him, "I am the LORD; and I appeared to Abraham, Isaac, and Jacob as God [EL] Almighty [SHADDAI], but by My name, LORD, **I did not make Myself known to them**." (Exodus 6:2-3).*

An easy explanation for the textual confusion is that Moses was the author of Genesis and simply used the Memorial Name in most of his narratives of the early patriarchs.

But let's get back to God's proclamation. In Hebrew, the proclamation of Exodus 34:6 begins (reading from the right):

אֵל יהוה יהוה

This can be rendered *"LORD, LORD, God."* The word "God" is our word *"EL"* in Hebrew.

TWICE

In Volume V of their Lexicon, Johannes Botterweck, Helmer Ringgren, and Heinz-Josef Fabry suggest that the four-character Memorial Name in Hebrew (יהוה) was derived from a three-consonant root that means to "be, become, come to pass" or simply, "I Am." Repeating the word twice gives the name great emphasis. In English we say things like, "I am very, very thankful" to emphasize how thankful we are. God's double Memorial Name thus could be rendered, "I Am that I Am" or the "Existent One, the

3 For more commentary, see the Exodus 6:3 discussion in *The Book of Exodus, Vol. 1*, of the New English Translation as edited by Rabbi Rosenberg.

"Eternal,"[4] or even "The One Who is, The One Who was, The One Who will be."

Spotlighting the fact that God's Memorial name is repeated twice in succession in verse six, the medieval French scholar and rabbi commonly known as Rashi (Shlomo Yitzchaki) provided this reflection in the 12th century: *"The one [occurrence] alludes to God having mercy on the sinner before he sins and the other after he has sinned and repented."* (Rosh Hashanah, 17b).

Rabbi Sforno had a different thought: *"...the One Who originates matters, called non-existent phenomena into existence. The repetition of the name a second time means that it is also He Who is eternal, not subject to fading into nothingness.... At the same time, it is He Who preserves these phenomena He called into existence."*[5]

Regardless of the meaning of the name itself, we can take the repetition as a sign of the LORD's greatness and His mercy.

The Hebrew word *El* in the proclamation takes us back to the Burning Bush account. Remember that it shows up there in its derivative plural form, **ELOHIYM**, which ties the Existent One back to the ancient patriarchs: Abraham, Isaac, and Jacob. The word **ELOHIYM** is used in the Burning Bush account five times. This is a very strong tie-back to a critical historical fact: God is already tied to Moses through prior covenants. Moses was in the direct line of a string of covenantal blessings upon Abraham and his offspring as were those who left Egypt with him.

When we think about what is being revealed in God's declaration to Moses, God's name says it all—a history involving every generation back to Adam and Eve. His name recalls His tendency to bind Himself to individuals. This

---

4 See Segonde's *La Sainte Bible* translation in Appendix A.

5 Commentary on the Torah by Rabbi Obadiah ben Jacob Sforno from Sefaria.org.

"Existent One, Existent One, God" is relational and faithful to His commitments. We will see this as we explore other words in the declaration.

Though a name is not the person it describes, it does refer that person to us in a special way. Even when a person is departed, a name can bring their presence to our minds. My mother and my father are deceased, but they are brought close to me whenever their name is spoken. This is particularly true when we hear an intimate reference to a parent. My father's name is Russell, but all the children and the grandchildren called him by his more intimate name, Papaw.

If we walk a long time with the LORD, even a reference to His Memorial Name can bring us into a form of communion. Because His Memorial Name appears over SIX THOUSAND times in the Hebrew Bible, there are plenty of additional attributes and nuances to excite our imagination and bring Him particularly close to our minds and hearts.

Let this fact sink deeply into your heart as we hear the proclamation of Who God is. You are overhearing an intimate revelation of His "name" and His consistent actions with mankind—with the children of Abraham and centuries later, with YOU!

CHAPTER FOUR

רַחוּם

RACHUWM
(COMPASSIONATE)

YHVH YHVH EL RACHUWM[6]

You can spot my car easily since my license plate is personalized with the Hebrew descriptive word, ***RACHUWM***. Why did I choose ***RACHUWM*** for my license plate? Because it is the first adjective describing God in Exodus 34:6. After the twice repeated Memorial Name of the LORD (***YHVH YHVH***) followed by the word ***EL*** for God, we immediately encounter the Hebrew adjective ***RACHUWM***. It is closely related to the Hebrew noun ***RECHEM*** that means "womb." ***RACHUWM*** and its related words occur in the Hebrew Bible over 100 times. ***RACHUWM*** describes someone with deep compassion and tender mercies.

---

6   In reverse order from Hebrew, i.e., written from left to right.

Perhaps you won't be surprised that **RACHUWM** is on my license plate since I frequently need to be reminded that I want to be compassionate toward others just like my Father in heaven is compassionate toward me.

Actually, if we really grasp the full meaning of this word, few of us probably would believe that God acts as **RACHUWM** suggests. Most of us view God primarily as the great Judge—the Punisher—One who metes out punishment on every side.

Instead, God comes to us with a deep underlying heart of compassion. For Him to choose the adjective **RACHUWM** to immediately follow His name tells us that it is of primary importance to Him as an attribute. This is good news and critical to remember.

WOMB

We can get a good idea of the meaning of **RACHUWM** through Isaiah's prophetic question as recorded in Isaiah 49:15: *"Can a woman forget her nursing child and have no compassion [RACHAM] on the son of her womb?"* **RACHAM**, a verb, is closely associated with our adjective, **RACHUWM**. We see **RACHAM** frequently translated as *"have compassion."* Further, it is paralleled with *"not forgetting,"* that is, being mindful and totally aware.

The passage tells us that God's compassion is even greater than that of a nursing mother. We can substitute "God" for "woman" in the passage and basically say, *"How can God forget the children He has birthed and fed; how can He not extend compassion to those He has created?"* The answer will be, *"He will not forget; He WILL extend compassion."*

Isaiah immediately follows with this amazing declaration:

"'Behold! I have gravened thee upon the palms of My hands; thy walls are continually before Me.'" (Isaiah 49:16, KJV).

GRAVEN

We must get personal or we will miss the point: "He will not forget YOU; YOUR name is engraved on the palm of His hand." He feels the greatest compassion for YOU! We then must ask the question, "Do I believe that?" Ninety-nine percent of us probably don't.

Fifteen years ago, I was walking across a field with mentor and friend, Dr. Terry Sanford Smith. Terry and I have walked together for over fifty years. He has been there in hard times and in times of joy. He is a counselor by vocation. Terry looked at me and asked, *"Rusty, did you know that God likes you?"*

I was startled by Terry's question. I knew unequivocally that God loved me in the Greek sense of *AGAPE* love (think John 3:16)[7], but LIKE me? I didn't think so—after all, how could He?

But God's *RACHUWM* shows a different side that is totally beyond me— He loves us with an even greater love and compassion than I have for my own children. God has compassion for ME! Since my children are virtually "graven upon the palms of my hands," I am engraved on His!

Does that mean He likes all of my mistakes? I don't think so. But His compassion—His *RACHUWM*—propels His heart toward me. And I, made in His image, desperately want His Spirit to propel me with compassion toward others just as He is propelled toward me!

HEARING THE CRY

God's compassion is like that of a mother who hears the cry of her child. King David wrote in Psalm 34:17-18:

---

7 *"For God so loved the world, that He gave His only Son, so that everyone who believes in Him will not perish but have eternal life."*

"The righteous cry, and the LORD hears and delivers them out of all their troubles. The LORD is near to the brokenhearted and saves those who are crushed in spirit."

Our 16th-century Rabbi Sforno connected this word, **RACHUWM**, not only to King David's psalm but also to Exodus 3:9 where God sees and sympathizes with the anguish of the downtrodden:

"Now, behold, the cry of the sons of Israel has come to Me; furthermore, I have seen the oppression with which the Egyptians are oppressing them."

Parents have a natural compassion toward their newly born, and it can be overwhelming. When Russell, our third child, was born, he spent many weeks in the neo-natal ICU. Robed in protective gear, I sat continuously by his side. His tiny hand instinctively gripped my index finger. I couldn't sleep, eat, think, or talk. My heart was breaking. There are not words to describe how captured I was by his plight. Deep compassion hits you like a sledgehammer.

Similar compassion can be triggered by the plight of an older child. Daughter Faith, our second child, was driving home from the University of Virginia when she reached down to change a CD. The car swerved slightly and went off Interstate 40, flipped three times, and landed in a ditch. Thirty minutes later, a Highway Patrol officer called to tell us there had been an accident. Regulations prevented him from disclosing her condition.

Fran and I were in total shock. We were five hours away from the accident. I couldn't breathe. My blood pressure went crazy. Without thinking, we immediately got into our car and drove to the scene of the wreck. All I can say now is that the compassion we felt for our daughter was not measurable. It was *beyond* beyond.

The same was true when our first child, Elizabeth, gave birth to Emmy, her fourth child. Again, we were brought to our knees. Unknowingly, Elizabeth had been bleeding internally for a full day after Emmy's arrival. White as the whitest sheet, she was going down fast. Gravely, the doctors explained that there was only a narrow chance of survival. We sat in an adjoining room in total shock. So much to lose; so much needed. Our hearts cried out to God.

Thankfully, all three of our children pulled through. But each crisis had sprung the wellspring of natural parental compassion.

One last example of parental compassion comes from the famous story of Solomon and the two women, one of whom lost their baby and one whose child survived. Both mothers claimed the living child as her own. When King Solomon tested their truthfulness, he proposed that the living child be split in two—one half for each mother. The mother of the living child, moved with great **RACHAM**, told Solomon to give the child to the other woman, thus revealing the depths of her compassion. Solomon immediately recognized that she was the true mother. Here we have compassion displayed even to the hurt of the one exhibiting compassion. (1st Kings 3:26).

What about on a broader front? Can we truly exhibit compassion toward those distant from us—those we don't naturally care for—those who have mistreated or abused us? What must occur? We certainly will need God's **RACHUWM**, His heart of compassion. Thankfully, Scriptures tell us that God will give Himself to those who seek after Him:

"You will seek Me and find Me when you search for Me with all your heart." (Jeremiah 29:13).

The Jeremiah passage reveals a wonderful promise. We *will* find God if we seek after Him, and finding Him, we will find a God of great Compassion. And if we truly find Him, we will want to devote ourselves entirely to Him. Consider this direction from Scripture:

"*Let your heart therefore be* **wholly** *devoted to the LORD God*" (1 Kings 8:61).

Yes, LORD, help us to fully devote our hearts to You! Over the years, my desire has grown to be wholly devoted to our Creator. My desire has been like a rudder—keeping me from wandering far off track. As each year has passed, my internal desire has grown stronger, more secure. Throughout the day, the thought keeps coming, "I want to be fully devoted to You." Fully devoted.

The famous Jewish Rabbi Moshe ben Maimon (known as Maimonides) rightly wrote, "*It is known and certain that the love of God does not become closely knit in a man's heart till he is continuously and thoroughly possessed by it and gives up everything else in the world for it. As God commanded us, 'with all your heart and with all your soul.'*" (see Deuteronomy 6:5 and the *Mishneh Torah*, Book I, Laws of Repentance, Ch. X.6).

Another important challenge is the transformation of our heart toward those around us, particularly those whom we naturally dislike. God sees the entire history of our fellow travelers, whereas we see only a dim view. We don't see their history of hurts and losses, the hidden tragedies, the abuse suffered during childhood. We see none of that, but God sees it all. Let us ask the God of the Universe to let us see as He sees. Hopefully our hearts will be filled with compassion—even toward our oppressors.

TWELVE TIMES IN ADDITION TO EXODUS 34:6

Including its presence in Exodus 34:6, the Hebrew word **RACHUWM** occurs in this exact form only thirteen times in Hebrew Scripture. It is only used in reference to God. In the twelve Scriptures below, Hebrew words repeated in Exodus 34:6-7 are in bold italic and inserted along with their related English words to make clear when the writer is using not only **RACHUWM** but also other words (or related words) from Exodus 34:6-7. As a reminder, here are all the transliterated Hebrew words straight from Exodus 34:6-7:

Va-ya'avor YHWH al-panav va-yikra
YHWH, YHWH el rachuwm v'channuwn erekh apayim v'rav
chesed v'emeth. Notser chesed la'alaphim nosei a-von
va-pesha v'chatta'ah v'naqei lo y'naqei poqed avon avot
al-banim v'al-banei vanim al-shilleshim v'al-ribe'im

Read each of the following verses slowly out loud and sit with it until you hear with your heart:[8]

"For the LORD your God [ELOHIYM] is a compassionate [RACHUWM] God [EL]; He will not fail you nor destroy you nor forget the covenant with your fathers [AVOT] which He swore to them."
(Deuteronomy 4:31)

"For if you return to the LORD, your brothers and your sons will find compassion [RACHAM] before those who led them captive and will return to this land. For the LORD your God [ELOHIYM] is gracious [CHANNUWN] and compassionate [RACHUWM] and will not turn His face away from you if you return to Him."
(2nd Chronicles 30:9)

---

8 The English translations are from the NASB.

"They refused to listen, And did not remember Your wondrous deeds
which You had performed among them; So they became stubborn and
appointed a leader to return to their slavery in Egypt. But You are a God of
forgiveness, Gracious [CHANNUWN] and compassionate [RACHUWM],
Slow [EREKH] to anger [APAYIM] and abounding [RAV] in
loving-kindness [CHESED]; And You did not forsake them."
(Nehemiah 9:17)

"Nevertheless, in Your great compassion [RACHAM]
You did not make an end of them or forsake them,
For You are a gracious [CHANNUWN]
and compassionate [RACHUWM] God [EL]."
(Nehemiah 9:31)

"But He, being compassionate [RACHUWM], forgave their iniquity
[AVON] and did not destroy them;
And often He restrained His anger [APAYIM]
And did not arouse all His wrath."
(Psalm 78:38)

"But You, O LORD, are a God [EL] merciful [RACHUWM]
and gracious [CHANNUWN],
Slow to anger [EREKH APAYIM] and abundant [RAV]
in loving-kindness [CHESED] and truth [EMETH]."
(Psalm 86:15)

"The LORD is compassionate [RACHUWM]
and gracious [CHANNUWN],
Slow to anger [EREKH APAYIM] and abounding [RAV]
in loving-kindness [CHESED]."
(Psalm 103:8)

"He has made His wonders to be remembered;
*The **LORD** is gracious [**CHANNUWN**]*
*and compassionate [**RACHUWM**]."*
(Psalm 111:4)

"Light arises in the darkness for the upright;
*He is gracious [**CHANNUWN**]*
*and compassionate [**RACHUWM**] and righteous."*
(Psalm 112:4)

*"The **LORD** is gracious [**CHANNUWN**]*
*and merciful [**RACHUWM**];*
*Slow to anger [**EREKH APAYIM**] and great [**RAV**]*
*in loving-kindness [**CHESED**]."*
(Psalm 145:8)

"'And rend your heart and not your garments.'
*Now return to the **LORD** your God [**ELOHIYM**],*
*For He is gracious [**CHANNUWN**]*
*and compassionate [**RACHUWM**],*
*Slow to anger [**EREKH APAYIM**],*
*abounding [**RAV**] in loving-kindness [**CHESED**]*
And relenting of evil."
(Joel 2:13)

*"He prayed to the **LORD** and said, "Please **LORD**, was not this what*
I said while I was still in my own country? Therefore, in order to forestall
*this, I fled to Tarshish, for I knew that You are a gracious [**CHANNUWN**]*
*and compassionate [**RACHUWM**] God [**ELOHIYM**], slow to anger*
*[**EREKH APAYIM**] and abundant [**RAV**] in loving-kindness [**CHESED**],*
and one Who relents concerning calamity."
(Jonah 4:2)

There are several things we can take from these thirteen verses. Obviously, later writers are sounding many of the same notes spoken by the Creator to Moses. In eleven verses, **RACHUWM** is linked closely to the next word we will study, the Hebrew word **CHANNUWN**, a word that means gracious—one who extends favor unconditionally. In our Exodus 34:6 verse, **RACHUWM** follows after the Memorial Name and comes immediately before the word **CHANNUWN**. One could say that God's Favor flows out of His Compassion in the original ordering. (See Exodus 34:6).

Consider carefully the preceding thirteen verses and you will see the original order of Exodus 34:6 is reversed eight out of eleven times. That is a bit surprising, but the words rhyme in Hebrew, and it may be a simple linguistic preference. The main point is that **RACHUWM** (compassionate) and **CHANNUWN** (gracious) are closely linked. Remember, a true heart of compassion leads to graciousness and kindness.

We can also note that the Joel 2:13 passage, Psalm 86:15, and Jonah 4:12 are almost exact duplicates of the declaration in Exodus 34:6, though only Psalm 86:15 picks up the word **EMETH**—the word for Truth.

You also will notice another frequent connection between **RACHUWM** and the word **CHESED** in six of the verses. We will look at that special connection in Chapter Seven which focuses on **CHESED**.

TRANSLATIONS

What about the potential translation confusion we have found in several of the most popular Bible translations? The Jewish Publication Society (JPS) 1917 translation, which is based on the Masoretic text, translates **RACHUWM** four times as *"merciful"* and nine times as *"compassionate"* or *"full of compassion."* The Modern English Translation of the Complete Tanakh (Bible) edited by Rabbi Rosenberg reverses the JPS and translates

RACHUWM ten times as *"merciful"* and only three times with the word *"compassionate."* The King James translates the word in our key text plus another seven instances as *"merciful,"* but uses *"compassion"* in five. The NASB and NIV are more consistent in translating *RACHUWM* as *"compassionate"* eleven times while using *"merciful"* twice. The RSV translates *RACHUWM* as *"merciful"* in Exodus 34:6 as well as eleven other occurrences while translating the word as *"compassionate"* in Psalm 78:38.

What gives? Undoubtedly, some of the confusion comes from translators who were influenced by a Greek translation dating from around 200 years before the Common Era. Current scholarship and the discovery of the Dead Sea scrolls have transformed earlier translations that were based on ancient Latin and Greek texts. Finally, there are simply doctrinal preferences. Check out the various translations in Appendix B. The first word after God will be the translator's choice for *RACHUWM*. My personal pick is Compassionate.

Let's sum up. God is amazingly compassionate—more compassionate than a nursing mother. He is tenderhearted toward ALL of His creation—propelled by compassion—gushing with compassion and mercy. We could say compassion is in His divine DNA! This is good news indeed!

CHAPTER FIVE

וְחַנּוּן

V-CHANNUWN
(GRACIOUS, KIND)

*YHVH YHVH EL RACHUWM **V'CHANNUWN**[9]*

GOOD NEWS AT THE BEGINNING

Right off the bat, we again have very good news. The ONE WHO IS, the EXISTENT ONE, יהוה, the LORD, revealed that He first comes with great compassion. Now, His heartfelt compassion moves naturally to the second characteristic, **CHANNUWN**. **CHANNUWN** is our word for gracious—showing undeserved favor and kindness.

---

9 In reverse order from Hebrew, i.e., written from left to right.

Let's remember. Moses had gone back up the mountain. It trembled and quaked at God's presence. Rockslides tumbled, lightning struck, and thunder pealed. A cloud or separation of some kind had enveloped Moses in a mountain crevice. He was sheltered there while God's presence was manifest. Moses heard a ringing proclamation in his own tongue: "*YHVH YHVH EL RACHUWM V'CHANNUWN....*" The LORD was directly answering Moses's important plea, "*Let me know Your ways that I may know You....*" *(Exodus 33:13).* He first came with a heart of great compassion. Now we learn that He also comes with *CHANNUWN*—most graciously—releasing mercy and favor on every side.

GOD'S HEART

God's heart precedes His actions. We could say His heart drives His actions. **CHANNUWN,** a Hebrew adjective, describes what He does: He acts with kindness and graciousness. If we want to have God-like kindness and graciousness with others, we must have a heart like His. Otherwise, we are only a cardboard caricature. LORD help us!

Think of this: since God is entirely *QODESH*, entirely OTHER, entirely BEYOND, isn't it amazing that the great God of the Universe would even meet with Moses? Just meeting with Moses is a sign of the LORD's *CHANNUWN*—His Graciousness.

The word itself contains a sense of both beauty and grace. Its primitive root, **CHANAN** (sometimes written as *HANAN* and pronounced *kha-nan'*), is a verb that means to show favor, extend grace and mercy. Close in meaning to the English word, "grace," and the Greek word *CHARIS*, it can also be used in an aesthetic sense (think rarified beauty). We say, "She is a graceful dancer," meaning that there is a rarified beauty in her movements.

The related root word, **CHANAH**, implies the action of bending or stooping. This colors the meaning of **CHANNUWN** with a sense of stooping in kindness to help a person of lesser rank.[10]

Closely related words occur many times in the Hebrew Bible, but like our word **RACHUWM, CHANNUWN** occurs only thirteen times and almost always in reference to the Creator. The first incidence happens earlier in Exodus when Moses recounts the instructions God gave him immediately prior to the Golden Calf episode. Another occurrence concerns a very practical rule for loaning protective personal items:

*"If you ever take your neighbor's cloak as a pledge, you are to return it to him before the sun sets, for that is his only covering; it is his cloak for his body. What else shall he sleep in? And it shall come about that when he cries out to Me, I will hear him, for I am gracious [**CHANNUWN**]."* (Exodus 22:26-27).

We see here something we noted about God's **RACHUWM**, His compassion. **CHANNUWN** is responsive to the "cry" of those in trouble. This is actually the only verse of the thirteen that does not mention the related idea of compassion specifically. But the word "cry" brings us back to the parental character of both words.

Still another occurrence that does not show up in our chapter on **RACHUWM** is from Psalms: *"Gracious [**CHANNUWN**] is the LORD, and righteous. Yes, our God is compassionate [**RACHAM**]."* (Psalm 116:5).

Aside from its appearance in Exodus 34:6-7, all other instances of **CHANNUWN** are partial repetitions of God's revelation to Moses on the mountain. We shared each of them in the preceding chapter on **RACHUWM**. God's compassion and grace are tied at the hip!

---

10   See Strong's H2583.

Let's unpack the word a bit further by looking at some striking characteristics.

GIFT

Grace carries with it the idea of gift. In other words, it is something you are not due. If you had earned whatever the action is that could be considered Grace, it is no longer Grace! You are simply being paid what was owed to you for your actions or your position. If you are a good girl, you get a treat. That is not Grace; that is what you were due for your actions. But if you are given a treat even after you have misbehaved, that is Grace.

The story of the Golden Calf is a perfect example of God's underlying tendency to bless and favor in spite of the fact that the Israelites were due no favor. Instead of abandoning them, the presence of God ended up going with them as they journeyed further. That was certainly a Grace as they had specifically broken covenant by doing the very thing they had promised not to do.

Many today are actually offended at the concept of Grace and can bring many objections to its extension in everyday circumstances. But I feel it is God's way to bend down to us—miracle of miracles—and extend favor when we certainly do not deserve it. In fact, the word "favor" carries with it the clear definition of something not owed. It is gratuitous, uncalled for, unwarranted.

GENEROSITY

But, if Grace is uncalled for, why is it being extended? There are several possibilities. The One extending Grace simply may be generous by nature. There is a good example of God going beyond what He is asked in His encounter with King Solomon:

"behold, I have done according to your words. Behold, I have given you a wise and discerning heart, so that there has been no one like you before you, nor shall one like you arise after you. ***I have also given you what you have not asked****, both riches and honor, so that there will not be any among the kings like you all your days."* (1ˢᵗ Kings 3:12-13).

I think also of Jesus of Nazareth's message to the crowds concerning their generosity and God's even greater generosity:

"Give, and it will be given to you; a good measure, pressed down, shaken together, and running over, will be poured into your lap. For with the measure you use, it will be measured back to you." (Luke 6:38; NIV).

This is an exuberant verse about giving—*running over*—overflowing! Thus, one of the possible reasons for God's Grace, His **CHANNUWN**, is that the God of the Universe is unbelievably generous.

LOVE

There is another possible reason for this undeserved Grace and Favor, and that is simply Love. It is an overused word in our culture—washed out in meaning. We need to draw back to the first time the ancient Hebrew word for love is used in the Bible.[11] It references Abraham's love for his dear son, Isaac. Isaac was a child promised to Abraham and Sarah in their old age. In a real sense, Isaac was Abraham's most precious possession. When we deeply love as Abraham loved, we will go way beyond giving what is due; we will give undeserved gifts.

My friend Bill once described God's loving nature by sharing a frequent happening in his household. In the evenings while his numerous children were doing their studies, Bill would ask if anyone wanted something from

---

11 See Genesis 22:2.

the refrigerator. A frequent answer would be a soda. Bill would return not only with a soda but also with a small bowl of fruit or even an ice cream sandwich. He felt God was exactly like that. God loves us unconditionally by nature, is attentive to our needs, and goes far beyond what is asked or needed.

MERCY

A third possibility is the concept we call Mercy—certainly one of the most direct meanings of the word, **CHANNUWN**. A tendency toward mercy means that when the weight of blame and innocence is perfectly balanced, one will choose mercy over punishment. In other words, God may simply be inclined toward mercy. We could say that it is because He is compassionate, deeply affectionate, and generous, but it could be that He simply is inclined toward mercy.

Rabbi Sforno's sixteenth-century commentary spotlights an aspect of God's mercy: God is even *"merciful to those who are guilty* [that is, deserving punishment], *reducing the punishment they really deserve...."*[12]

Victor Hugo in his book, *Les Misérables,* has a scene that has stuck in my memory. Really, it is a most perfect example of **CHANNUWN** in all of its fullness. Jean Valjean, recently released after nineteen years of imprisonment, had found shelter one evening at the home of a stranger, the Monseigneur Bienvenu.[13]

Treated to an undeserved and elaborate dinner the night of his welcome, Jean Valjean awoke in the middle of the night, stole six sets of silverware belonging to the Monseigneur, and departed immediately under the cover

---

12 https://www.sefaria.org/Sforno_on_Exodus.34.6.4

13 The French word *Bienvenu* appropriately means "welcome" in English.

of darkness. Spotted rushing away, he was arrested by three gendarmes and taken back to the priest's home.

Instead of demanding the return of his silver, the Monseigneur walked over to his fireplace mantle and removed the last two things of value in his modest home: two silver candlesticks. Turning to Jean Valjean in front of the gendarmes, he exclaimed,

"'I am glad to see you! Well, but how is this? I gave you the candlesticks too, which are of silver like the rest, and for which you can certainly get two hundred francs. Why did you not carry them away with your forks and spoons?'... Jean Valjean was like a man on the point of fainting. The Bishop drew near to him and said in a low voice: 'Do not forget, never forget, that you have promised to use this money to become an honest man.'

"Jean Valjean, who had no recollection of ever having promised anything, remained speechless. The Bishop had emphasized the words when he uttered them. He resumed with solemnity: 'Jean Valjean, my brother, you no longer belong to evil, but to good. It is your soul that I buy from you; I withdraw it from black thoughts and the spirit of perdition, and I give it to God.'"

Here we have punishment due, a remittance of punishment, PLUS a totally gratuitous addition of an undeserved benefit.

Whether it is God's immeasurable inclination to generosity, His deep love, His mercy, or all three, we can trust that His inclination to go beyond what we are due is good news indeed!

TRANSLATIONS

We find greater consistency in the way various versions handle **CHANNUWN**. Unlike the King James Bible's inconsistency in translating the word **RACHUWM**, the NASB, the JPS (1917) and the *Modern English*

Translation of the Complete Tanakh as edited by Rabbi Rosenberg are very consistent, translating the word as *"gracious"* in all thirteen instances. The NIV and RSV translate **CHANNUWN** as *"compassionate"* once in Exodus 22:27 but use *"gracious"* the rest of the time. On the whole, there is a great deal of support for the word Gracious.

SUMMING UP

Since we are all made in His image, one of the most important takeaways for **CHANNUWN** is that this special attribute should be ours as well. We are made for it! But an even casual review of our individual situations will likely reveal that the Grace we extend to others falls significantly short. We can be so dominated by our personal needs that we give little thought to how we can bless others. May our gracious Lord help us!

CHAPTER SIX

אֶרֶךְ אַפַּיִם [14]

EREKH APAYIM
(SLOW TO ANGER)

YHVH YHVH EL RACHUWM V'CHANNUWN
EREKH APAYIM[15]

Good news again for Moses and for us. The God of the Universe is slow to anger! Moses is crouched in the cleft of the rock and has already received two surprising revelations about Who God is. Now, he gets a third. From a relational point of view, this attribute is a zinger. Intimate relationships can be tragically marred and even destroyed by anger.

---

14 Words in Hebrew, that is, written right to left.

15 Words in reverse order from Hebrew, that is, written from left to right.

In this context, **EREKH** means "slow," and **APAYIM** means "to anger." **APAYIM** has an interesting etymological history; it basically comes from a word referencing parts of the body and the nose in particular. When the word is pronounced, you get a physical sense of someone truly angry. Try saying the word out loud with gusto. **APAYIM!** I think of a cartoon character from my childhood Saturday morning TV shows: ole Yosemite Sam. For readers who weren't born seventy-five years ago, Yosemite Sam was the gunslinging nemesis of Bugs Bunny.

An angry guy if ever there was one.

Thankfully, Yosemite Sam is NOT a caricature of our Creator! Combined with the Hebrew word **EREKH** (which means lengthen or delay), we have the idea of slowing down the **APAYIM**, the anger. Thus, *"slow to anger."*

God presents Himself in this third characteristic as being able to put up with hurtful behavior for a long time. Some Hebrew sages saw this as flowing from God's compassion—the hope that the one hurting another would cease from hurting and turn to kindness.

The Hebrew prophet, Habakkuk, could say of the LORD, *"Your eyes are too pure to approve evil, and You cannot look on wickedness with favor,"* and yet ask, *"Why do You look with favor on those who deal treacherously? Why are You silent when the wicked swallow up those more righteous than they?"* (Habakkuk 1:13). Instead of intervening to stop the wicked quickly, God delays in order to give the wicked an opportunity for remorse and provides them space to turn away from their hurtful behavior on their own.

Rabbi Kaufmann Kohler, Rabbi Emeritus of Temple Beth-El in New York, agreed: *"God's anger is never the outburst of a mere capricious passion, but is a necessary element of His moral order. 'Fury is not in me.' (Isaiah 27:4). It is restrained and controlled by divine mercy, the correlate attribute of justice."*[16]

Thus, we see the first characteristic, **RACHUWM**, working with the third characteristic, **EREKH APAYIM**. The psalmist Asaph declared, *"But He, being compassionate [**RACHUWM**], forgave their iniquity and did not destroy them; and **often He restrained His anger** and did not arouse all His wrath."* (Psalm 78:38).

In personal dealings, being slow to anger is a great blessing.

*"He who is slow [**EREKH**] to anger [**APAYIM**]*
is better than the mighty,
And he who rules his spirit,
than he who captures a city."
(Proverbs 16:32).

THE VIRTUE OF ANGER

The Creator has given every one of us the ability to be angry. Mankind, along with the higher-level animal kingdom, has been given two protective impulses: fight and flight. The amygdala, that part of our brain that helps process threats and losses, sends signals to our hypothalamus. Those signals trigger involuntary functions that increase our oxygen intake, blood pressure, temperature, and heart function. This heightens our capacity to

---

16   From the entry on *Anger* in the 1906 Jewish Encyclopedia.

deal with a variety of environmental and emotional threats, hurts, and serious difficulties. It allows razor focus on what is immediately before us.

Unfortunately, the physiological side effects can be quite dangerous. In the heat of the moment, our attention is so narrowed and so directed that broader information processing is skewed—our judgment impaired. We may do and say things that we normally would know to be dead wrong. The negative repercussions can be enormous.

Think for a moment of a simple example. You are driving a car. Another car pulls up alongside. The driver's window is down, and he casts a racial slur toward you. Incensed, you shout back, taking your eyes off the road for a moment. The intersection ahead becomes your death trap, and you crash into a car you would have otherwise avoided.

But the reverse can be true. Imagine yourself a teacher. You see a much smaller boy being bullied by a teenage boy several years senior and significantly larger in size. Anger can give you the adrenaline and focus to intervene even though the older child is larger than you. Anger in this case can stop injustice.

The first case is focused entirely on the angry person's identity and his concern for himself and his status. The second case mimics God's normal intervention behind much of what we would call God's *APAYIM*. The exhaustive 1901 edition of *The Jewish Encyclopedia* points out that God's anger is *"kindled not only by **idolatry** (Deuteronomy 6:15; 9:19; 29:17; … and elsewhere), by **rebellion** (Numbers 11:1), **ingratitude** (Numbers 11:10), **disregard of things holy** (Numbers 17:13, 16:4,7; Leviticus 10:6; Numbers 25:3; 2ⁿᵈ Samuel 6:7; Isaiah 5:25) and **disobedience** (Exodus 4:14), but also by the **oppression of the poor** (Exodus 22:23; Isaiah 9:16; 10:4)."*

Let's spotlight these six actions and attitudes that provoke the Almighty:

Idolatry

Rebellion

Ingratitude

Disregard of Things Holy (things that are **QODESH**)

Disobedience

Oppression of the Poor (Injustice)

God's anger is released to stop that which should not be. Let me repeat that one more time: **Anger is released to stop that which should not be.** Bishop Robert Barron rightly commented that the word "anger" is a *"metaphor to express God's passion to set things right."* (*Word on Fire*, 2020.11.29). God's concern is never for Himself. In other words, righteous anger is deployed to still the destructive consequences of bad behavior from increasing.

> *"For wickedness burns like a fire;*
> *It consumes briars and thorns;*
> *It even sets the thickets of the forest aflame."*
> (Isaiah 9:18).

God-like anger is never released to "get back at," return a hurt, or gain selfish advantage. Unfortunately, in both our personal interactions and our national politics, anger is most frequently deployed with at least one of these three aims in mind.

Regarding God's anger over Ingratitude, I am reminded of the 2nd-century theologian, Irenaeus of Lyons (130-202 AD). I believe Irenaeus would have said that God does not "need" our gratitude. God desires our gratefulness because of what that virtue does for ourselves and those around us. We know from Scripture that God's ire *IS* raised when one has been shown great mercy and grace and then is unwilling to extend the same to his or her neighbor. Hurtful behavior can provoke God to action because of its effect on others. Like Irenaeus, I don't believe God "needs" anything!

Maimonides concurred, "...*all beings are in need of Him; but He, blessed be He, is not in need of them nor of any one of them. Hence, His real essence is unlike that of any of them.*" (*Basic Principles of the Torah*, Chapter 1.3).

BITTERNESS

Most dangerous is harboring unrighteous anger—keeping it in. In the New Testament *Book of Hebrews*, the author admonishes: "*Pursue peace with all men, and the sanctification without which no one will see the Lord. See to it that no one comes short of the grace of God; that no root of bitterness springing up causes trouble, and by it many be defiled....*" (Hebrews 12:14-15). This clearly recalls a portion from Deuteronomy 29:18, "*that there will not be among you a root bearing poisonous fruit and wormwood.*"

Bitterness is a cancer that comes from harboring anger for hurts received, either by you or someone close to you. Many a relationship, workplace, synagogue, or church community has been defiled by harbored unrighteous anger on the part of one or two. Like the Wormwood plant (*Artemisia absinthium*) which can cause convulsions and even death, bitterness has such toxicity that it can destroy relationships if left to fester.

Wormwood

Over my last fifty years, I have witnessed multiple incidences of relational collapse caused by long-harbored anger and bitterness. One situation in particular comes to mind. A man lost a dear sister from a dreadful disease. The husband of the man's sister quickly remarried. Though the two men had been close friends prior to the loss, the wife's brother felt his sister had been dishonored and devalued. Bitterness grew in the man's heart until it became all consuming. Though family members tried to intervene, every effort was rebuffed. The estrangement continued for years with great loss.

Harbored anger appears to be placid on the surface, but underneath is a boiling cauldron ready to explode. The only answers are to either let it go (which also can be dangerous) or have it dissolved by compassion and grace. The latter is the real answer. Lord, help us!

NOT LONG

Thankfully, the Lord's anger, when it does arise, lasts but for a moment:

> *"For His anger [**APAYIM**] is but for a moment,*
> *His favor is for a lifetime;*
> *Weeping may last for the night,*
> *But a shout of joy comes in the morning."*
> (Psalm 30:5).

This is consistent with Isaiah 54:8:

> *"In an outburst of anger*
> *I hid My face from you for a moment,*
> *But with everlasting loving-kindness [**CHESED**]*
> *I will have compassion [**RACHAM**] on you."*

The Prophet Isaiah links three of our proclamation attributes together and tells us why God doesn't leave anger hanging. His Anger *[APAYIM]* lasts only a moment because of His everlasting Loving-kindness *[CHESED]* and His Compassion *[RACHAM]*.

God has given us the ability to move out of anger quickly. Unfortunately, most of us grow up relishing the power and sense of justification that we feel when we are angry. But anger needs to be quickly overcome by compassion and loving-kindness so that the rational part of our brains can take over. Isaiah says, *"for a moment."* That is a good rule *every* time we find ourselves incited to anger.

SUMMING UP

This is all good news. And imagine how good it was from Moses's point of view. Only a few days earlier, Moses had burned with anger to such a degree that he broke the precious tablets inscribed supernaturally by the LORD. In Exodus 34:6-7, our Creator is teaching Moses how a Godly response differs from responding to uncontrolled impulses. But our two words, *EREKH APAYIM*, precede an even more stabilizing characteristic of God—His *CHESED*.

CHAPTER SEVEN

וְרַב־חֶסֶד

V'RAV CHESED
(ABUNDANT IN LOVING-KINDNESS)

YHVH YHVH EL RACHUWM CHANNUWN EREKH APAYIM
V'RAV CHESED[17]

Abounding! Our little three Hebrew character word **RAV** is a contraction of the Hebrew word that means "to multiply by the myriad!" The God of the universe is ABOUNDING to the nth degree in the quality of **CHESED**.[18] I don't have words to express how important **CHESED** is.

---

17 Words in reverse order from Hebrew, that is, written from left to right.

18 *CHESED* is pronounced differently than it may appear. Instead of the CH being pronounced like the "ch" in challenge, it is pronounced with a slight rasp in the back of the throat—as the "ch" at the end of Bach. Another approach is to give it a hard "H" like heh-SED.

There is an underlying characteristic of **CHESED** that cannot be measured. Scriptures say over and over that it never comes to an end. **CHESED** turned me on my heels as I mentioned in the Preface. It was fifty years ago when I read Norman Snaith's little book and began to focus on distinctive ideas in early Hebrew Scripture. They were distinctive enough to cause me to have a personalized license plate in the 1970s emblazoned with **CHESED**. It was the quality I most wanted in my life and one that I thought was far from me. It still is. Perhaps its value will become clearer as we go along.

V'RAV CHESED! Abounding in Loving-kindness, Steadfast Love, Loyal Love, Devoted Love, Faithful Love, Covenant Love! All of these relational expressions touch some of the word's essence. It is an amazingly deep word that plunges us into the depths of our Creator's heart.

Remember that **CHESED** is a relational term. In fact, all of God's characteristics in Exodus 34:6-7 are relational. The Creator is addressing how He *relates* in a relationship, whether with an individual or an entire nation. God can be fully counted on to come to your aid with force and power. Even when you have stretched His patience to the limit (if there is such a point), He can still be counted on. In other words, God is entirely Faithful. Not wishy-washy. Solid.

We are on sacred ground here, and the more we dig, the more sacred the word appears.

TOUGH

This is not some namby-pamby, weak-kneed God with Whom we are dealing. This is the Creator of the Universe, powerful beyond imagination. And the nature of His **CHESED** reflects toughness and strength. "Steadfast" really means tough—something we can count on no matter what. We had an old saying in the U.S. Marines: "*When the going gets tough, the tough get* *going."* We meant that no matter how bad the situation was, a Marine had to have the fortitude to come against it with all of his might.

We start with the thought of God's underlying toughness because so many definitions instead begin with His love. **CHESED** does mean a unique type of love that the English language is challenged to describe with one word. Most of us do not think of toughness when we hear the word "love." But toughness is a critical component of **CHESED**.

My go-to meaning for **CHESED** over the last forty years still stands: "A stubborn determination to remain faithful in a relationship, no matter what!" Traditionally, we have expressed this in the vows of marriage: *"for better, for worse, for richer, for poorer, in sickness and in health."* Staying faithful in a relationship when things are "worse" requires a level of toughness.

Lest we forget, keep toughness in mind as we dive further.

FAITHFUL

Closely tied to the characteristic of Toughness is the characteristic of Faithfulness that **CHESED** boldly manifests.

"I will sing of the loving-kindness [CHESED] of the LORD forever; To all generations I will make known Your faithfulness with my mouth." (Psalm 89:1).

A faithful person can be entirely counted on when the going gets rough. It is easy to be alongside another when times are good; real faithfulness is revealed when times are terrible. Think of your own personal difficulties with others, often with those closest to you. Most marriages fail because people just can't or don't keep going when things get rough. Over **40 percent** of American "first" marriages end in divorce. And that is after almost all who get married publicly promise to never fail or leave their spouse.

STICKY

The God of the Universe is sticky, that is, tenacious. He is inclined to stick with those with whom He relates in spite of great difficulty. This is a critical aspect of **CHESED**: a willingness to stick to someone no matter what, in spite of SEVERE disappointment, rejection, and even terrible behavior. The Book of Proverbs spotlights this aspect: *"One who has unreliable friends soon comes to ruin, but there is a friend who sticks closer than a brother."* (Proverbs 18:24, *NIV*). God tilts toward sticking with us. For one thing, He is willing to wait a LONG TIME for positive change in the relationship, no matter whether His relationship is with a people like Israel or a person like Aaron. Or a person like Moses. Or a person like me! Or a person like YOU!

Immediately before His proclamation to Moses, the Creator had proved that **CHESED** was a deep part of His nature by sticking with the children of Israel in their outright rebellion.

If you are pushing back at this point—imagining that anyone, much less the God of the Universe—could be like this, and even more wondering how being like this could make any practical sense at all, my response is that I truly believe that this is the way God is and the way He wants us to be. Really, it reflects God's similar tendency to fall *toward* grace *(CHANNUWM)* as opposed to judgment when the scales are balanced between the two actions.

There are conditions when God's stickiness becomes unstuck. We will dive into them in Chapter Ten. But God's heart is always for reconciliation. He is the God of reconciliation. He longs for it, prepares for it, does all that He can to cause it.

KARATH BERIYTH

One of the most remarkable expressions of **CHESED** is God's willingness to enter into binding covenants—with both mankind and all living creatures. He has entered into many, including:

- With mankind and Noah. (Genesis 9:1-17).

- With Abraham; the covenant that is called *Brit bein HaBetarim*, that is, the *Cutting of the Pieces.* (Genesis 15:1-21).

- With Abraham that is called the *Brit Milah*, that is, the *Cutting of Circumcision.* (Genesis 17:11-13).

- With Isaac in Genesis 17:19.

- With Jacob (Israel) in Leviticus 26:42.

- With Moses and the Children of Israel; that is called the *Brit Sinai.* (Exodus 34:10)

- With Aaron and the Priesthood, which is called the *Brit ha-Kehuna.* (Numbers 18:19).

- With Phinehas in a covenant of peace. (Numbers 25:11-12)

- With King David. (2nd Samuel 7:8-17 and 2nd Samuel 23:5).

- And a "new" promised covenant, *Brit Hadasha* [בְּרִית חֲדָשָׁה], with the tribes of Israel and Judah. (Jeremiah 31:31). Christians believe that this last one, as prophesied by the Prophet Jeremiah, was fulfilled at the death of Jesus of Nazareth. Portions of the key verses are repeated verbatim in the Book of Hebrews as recorded there in Chapters Eight, Nine, and Ten.

This willingness of the Creator to enter into binding covenants is extraordinary. It will be even more so when we drill down into the true meanings behind our English words for making a covenant. Plus, a covenant is closely associated with the meaning of **CHESED**. **CHESED** is needed in every covenant. **CHESED** undergirds covenant, and every covenant needs **CHESED** in order to last.

The late Englishman Jonathan Sacks, former Chief Rabbi of the United Hebrew Congregation of the Commonwealth, focused on the intimate relationship between **CHESED** and the Hebrew word for covenant, **BERIYTH** (also written as **BRIT** and **BERIT**), when he said, *"God will never break the covenant, even if we do, because of His* **CHESSED** *[sic]."*[19]

The word **BERIYTH** is frequently translated as "covenant" and occurs over two hundred and eighty times in the Hebrew Bible. In English, the word actually means "cutting." Along with its normal companion word, **KARATH**, the entire phrase means "cut a cutting" or "cut a separation." In ancient compacts, what is cut is flesh, and what issues forth is blood. This means the Ark of the Covenant in one sense is the Ark of the Cutting. For Jewish males, being "circumcised" is being cut—being separated unto God—an act of entering into God's covenant; a **BRIT**. For most people who dig down to this level of semantics, that puts an entirely new spin on the word "covenant," making it a matter of life and death, flesh and blood.

A most important concept, Hebrew Scripture associates the word **BERIYTH** with God's proclamation word, **CHESED**. Grasping this relationship spotlights being bound to someone else—in this case the Creator's binding to mankind and to individual people.

Rabbi Sacks continues, *"A* **BRIT** *is made when free agents, respecting one another's freedom, bind themselves by a mutual promise to work together,*

19 https://rabbisacks.org/eikev-5780/.

to be loyal to one another, and to achieve together what neither can achieve alone."

But why "cutting?" Remember, what is cut is flesh, and what pours forth is blood. Early Middle Eastern people rightly understood that "life was in the blood." (see Leviticus 17:11). Remove the flow of blood from our internal organs, and our organs die in short order. Ancient tribes and cultures all over the world used the action of cutting flesh, whether human, bird, or animal, to symbolize the severe seriousness of entering into a binding agreement. In some cases, animals were cut in pieces, and the participants who were being bound to a sovereign agreement would walk between the pieces. What they were saying to each other was, "So should it be done to me if I break this covenant!"

One of the most astounding sections of Scripture is the scene in Genesis between God and Abraham:

"He said, 'O Lord GOD, how may I know that I will possess it?' So, He said to him, 'Bring Me a three-year-old heifer, and a three-year-old female goat, and a three-year-old ram, and a turtledove, and a young pigeon.' Then he brought all these to Him and cut them in two and laid each half opposite the other; but he did not cut the birds. The birds of prey came down upon the carcasses, and Abram drove them away. Now when the sun was going down, a deep sleep fell upon Abram; and behold, terror and great darkness fell upon him.... It came about when the sun had set, that it was very dark, and behold, there appeared a smoking oven and a flaming torch which passed between these pieces. On that day the LORD made a covenant with Abram, saying, 'To your descendants I have given this land, From the river of Egypt as far as the great river, the river Euphrates....'" (Genesis 15:8-12,17-18).

What happened in this cutting is that the God of the Universe stooped down in symbolic form to enter into and use a cultural practice known to Abraham to "bind" the compact. Most astounding!

This sign in Abraham's day sealed the covenant by blood. Another vivid example of a **Brit bein HaBetarim** *(Cutting of the Pieces)* is recorded in Jeremiah 34:18-19. It recalls a covenant entered into with the tribe of Judah and Jerusalem:

"the covenant which they made before Me, when they cut the calf in two and passed between its parts, the officials of Judah and the officials of Jerusalem, the court officers and the priests and all the people of the land who passed between the parts of the calf."

Rabbi Rashi in commenting on Jeremiah 34:18 said that the cutting of an animal in two parts and passing between the pieces was stating to the covenant parties that, *"So shall the one who transgresses be cut and divided."*[20]

The shedding of blood is both a sign of life and of death. It is consistently used frequently throughout Scripture as the sign of the binding of wills, that is, the cutting *(KARATH)* of a covenant *(BERIYTH)*. *CHESED* seals the compact.

"O LORD, the God of Israel, there is no God like You in heaven above or on earth beneath, keeping covenant [BERIYTH] and showing loving-kindness [CHESED] to Your servants who walk before You with all their heart...." (1ˢᵗ Kings 8:23).

"Now therefore, our God, the great, the mighty, and the awesome God, Who keeps covenant [BERIYTH] and loving-kindness [CHESED]...." (Nehemiah 9:32).

---

20 Rashi's Commentary on Jeremiah 34:18 in the *Tanakh.*

*"My loving-kindness [**CHESED**] I will keep for him forever,*
*And My covenant [**BERIYTH**] shall be confirmed to him."* (Psalm 89:23).

"Incline your ear and come to Me. Listen, that you may live; And I will make
*[**KARATH**] an everlasting covenant [**BERIYTH**] with you, according to the*
*faithful mercies [**CHESED**] shown to David."* (Isaiah 55:3).

The Isaiah passage referenced above reminds us of the covenantal aspect of **CHESED** displayed by David immediately after he had become king following the death of King Saul and his son, Jonathan. Though Jonathan had been in line to succeed Saul, David had entered into a binding covenant with Jonathan while he was alive. Middle Eastern monarchs would normally have killed the relatives of a preceding king who could have advanced claims to the throne, but because of the covenant David had made, we find him seeking to express **CHESED** to any of Jonathan's living relatives.

"The king (DAVID) said, 'Is there not yet anyone of the house of Saul to
*whom I may show the kindness [**CHESED**] of God?' And Ziba said to the*
king, 'There is still a son of Jonathan who is crippled in both feet.'" (2nd Samuel 9:3).

Because of the **CHESED** in David, Jonathan's son Mephibosheth was brought to live in King David's house, treated with dignity and honor, and given the lands his grandfather had owned.

"For the mountains may be removed and the hills may shake, But My lov-
*ing-kindness [**CHESED**] will not be removed from you, And My covenant*
*[**BERIYTH**] of peace will not be shaken,' Says the LORD Who has compas-*
*sion [**RACHAM**] on you."* (Isaiah 54:10).

This verse from Isaiah highlights that it is not simply loving-kindness or steadfast love that triggers and animates God's binding. This willingness to bind also stems from His compassion. However, the main thrust is **CHESED.**

CHESED's connection with creation and the maintenance of covenantal relationships brings us to another characteristic: saltiness.

SALTY/STEADFAST

SALT BLOCK

*"All the offerings of the holy gifts, which the sons of Israel offer to the LORD, I have given to you and your sons and your daughters with you, as a perpetual allotment. It is an everlasting covenant [**BERIYTH**] of **salt** before the LORD to you and your descendants with you."* (Numbers 18:19).

Salt was and is a symbol of integrity—something that lasts, something that has the capacity to preserve and bring benefits. Chemically, sodium ions and chloride ions bind together. One sodium atom is able to provide the extra electron needed by the chlorine atom to make a tight bond between the two. The combination of sodium, chloride, and other trace minerals helps livestock avoid dehydration and promotes digestion and assimilation of food. A lack of minerals in the diet leads to low meat and milk productivity and decreased fertility.

These special qualities made salt a perfect symbol of covenantal binding. I connect it directly to the quality of **CHESED**—a willingness to endure in difficult situations and not be corrupted—the quality of integrity. Outside, a salt block must endure hostile weather and hold together. It must maintain its INTEGRITY, its ability to remain STEADFAST—a fundamental characteristic of *CHESED*.

Unfortunately,

> *"Many a man proclaims his own loyalty [**CHESED**],*
> *But who can find a trustworthy man?"*
> (Proverbs 20:6).

It has been over forty-five years since I began to focus on the preceding proverb. It fueled a desire in me to be trustworthy, that is, a man of integrity. But like salt from the Middle East, it is not manufactured by effort. Native people find salt in nature and rightly consider it a gift from God. The same is true for men and women who want to have lives full of *CHESED*. It really is a God-gift if one can receive it.

Having the God quality of *CHESED* in us is extremely important to God:
> *"For I delight in loyalty [**CHESED**] rather than sacrifice,*
> *And in the knowledge of God rather than burnt offerings."*
> (Hosea 6:6).

Be on the lookout for examples of steadfastness in the lives of others and celebrate it. I have a friend with whom I have worked for over fifty years. His wife had a terrible stroke six years ago. My friend quit work and went home to care for her. Many would have hired help, but something in my friend wanted to give himself to her care completely. He ministers to her needs day and night; he lifts her from wheelchair to couch; he does everything required. A great sportsman, he gave up his favorite pursuit. He has remained STEADFAST. His actions have proved himself to be "a trustworthy man," a man of *CHESED*.

We also have the amazing example of Ruth, the Moabite widow who was the great-grandmother of King David. During a severe famine in Israel, Ruth's Jewish mother-in-law, Naomi, had immigrated with her husband and two sons to the country of Moab. The Moabites were traditional enemies of Israelites, so you can imagine the disdain when both of her sons married women from Moab. Naomi's husband died tragically in Moab along with her two sons. Despondent, Naomi wanted to return to Israel after the death of the three men. Ruth and Ruth's sister-in-law accompany her to the border of Israel at which point the sister-in-law returns to Moab. Naomi encourages Ruth to return as well, afraid that Ruth will be an outcast in a foreign land. But Ruth is sticky; she is filled with **CHESED**. Her response to Naomi is one of my favorite verses in the entire Bible—one that I repeated verbatim to my wife Fran at our rehearsal dinner forty-seven years ago:

"Do not plead with me to leave you or to turn back from following you; for where you go, I will go, and where you sleep, I will sleep. Your people shall be my people, and your God, my God. Where you die, I will die, and there I will be buried." (Ruth 1:16).

May the **CHESED** of Ruth be in each of us. And may we receive the gift of God's steadfastness!

EVERLASTING

Our Creator's **CHESED** lasts forever. This is affirmed over and over in the Scriptures. This too is good news. It never comes to an end.

"O give thanks to the LORD, for He is good;
*For His loving-kindness [**CHESED**] is **everlasting**."*
(1st Chronicles 16:34).

"For the LORD is good;
*His loving-kindness [**CHESED**] is **everlasting***
And His faithfulness to all generations."
(Psalm 100:5).

One of my favorite songs for times of worship is lifted verbatim from the King James version of *Lamentations*, Chapter 3, verses 22-23. It expresses this truth beautifully, adding a flavor of compassion to the reflection:

*"The Steadfast Love [**CHESED**] of the Lord **never ceases;***
*His mercies [**RACHAM**] **never come to an end.***
They are new every morning. Great is YOUR faithfulness!"

This verse occurs in the middle of *Lamentations,* a book filled with sorrows and woe. It connects not only to real life but also to God's faithfulness no matter how difficult our circumstances may be. Remember, no matter how hard things are in the present, God's Steadfast Love and Mercy never come to an end!

LOVING AND KIND

CHESED is full of love and kindness. I purposely have chosen to focus on these two characteristics last in order to emphasize the other remarkable characteristics of God's **CHESED**. Love and Kindness complete the circuit. There is a zealousness to the Love that **CHESED** drives, and we see that its zeal produces action. It is not an abstract word. It is demonstrated and proven in action.

The Greek word that underlies the heart of Christian Scripture is the word **AGAPE**. In ancient Greece, there were three words that characterized different types of Love: **PHILEO, EROS**, and **AGAPE. PHILEO** is the love shown between friends, **EROS** the word that describes carnal love, and

AGAPE a love that is demonstrated by costly sacrifice. I believe *AGAPE* is the type of love that most closely resembles *CHESED*. It, too, is a love proven in action—a love not just expressed because of duty or obligation, but a love that springs from the deepest affection—the love of a parent for a beloved child—a love that will cause one to give his or her own life for the beloved. As a Christian, it is this love that the Apostle John is describing in the third chapter of his Gospel.

A remarkably broad term, one might say that *CHESED* contains all of the other attributes described in Exodus 34:6-7.

TRANSLATIONS

The Modern English Translation of the Complete Tanakh as edited by Rabbi Rosenberg translates *CHESED* in Exodus 34:6-7 as *"Loving-kindness."* The NASB follows suit, though less frequently. It uses **Kindness** and on rare occasions the word **Mercy**. **Kindness** reminds us of our related word, *CHANNUWN*. Interestingly, the King James Version translates *CHESED* seventy-five percent of the time as **Mercy**, though in Exodus 34:6-7, it uses the word **Goodness**. Exhaustive studies by Botterweck, Ringgren, and Green suggest, however, that *CHESED* is closer to a constant **Kindness** or **Goodness** than it is to **Mercy**. As mentioned in Chapter Two, this may be because the Greek Septuagint version of the Hebrew Scriptures translated by ancient Jewish Scholars before the first century most often translated *CHESED* with the Greek word ἔλεος *(ELEOS)*—the Greek word for **Mercy**.

No doubt, *ELEOS* had a great influence on early translators. After our study of *CHANNUWN*, this might surprise you (as it did me) since I believe a very close translation of *CHANNUWN* would be the word **Mercy**. Interestingly, modern-day Jewish scholars in the JPS (1917) translated the first *CHESED* in our proclamation by using the word **Goodness**.

The second time around, they used the word **Mercy**. In the 1999 update, the Jewish Publication Society switched to **Kindness** for both occurrences in Exodus 34:6-7.

Other translations use other words. The English Standard Version (EVS) translated it as "**Steadfast Love**." The 1978 version of my favorite French Bible uses the French word *Bienveillance* that basically means **Benevolence**.

My personal favorite English translation for **CHESED** is **Steadfast Love**, but no matter what my favorite is, I am thankful God is overflowing in **CHESED**. May we be as well!

SUMMING UP

Perhaps you grasp at this point that I am an enthusiastic fan of the idea that **CHESED** emanates from God. Can't you see me in the stands waving a placard emblazoned with the word, **CHESED**? Yes, that would be me.

Let me tell you a story of how wonderful it is when you can experience **CHESED** in your everyday relationships. **CHESED** is a gift from God—part of Who He is and part of the image He has placed within each one of us. Our challenge is to unlock it.

Years ago, I had the distinct pleasure of beginning a **CHESED** relationship with a friend who unfortunately is no longer with us. His name was John. I had done nothing to deserve the pleasure of that relationship; it was simply a God-gift from my point of view. We had lunch together every Tuesday. There was no agenda; we simply enjoyed being together. Both of us had children and spouses that we dearly loved, and often we spent our time telling stories about special things the children had done or were doing. We talked about the past, we talked about the present, and we talked about the future. We were, so far as I know, entirely transparent with one another.

I felt safe in John's presence, and I believe he felt safe in mine. We had no plans to "fix" each other.

When John was in his late fifties, he developed a terrible *glioblastoma* brain tumor. John was stricken physically, and I was stricken emotionally. During a long season of treatment, I hovered alongside his dear family, wrote a daily update blog for John's friends, researched national cancer centers, and simply tried to stay close. The nature of the relationship between us, its **CHESED**, was no longer expressed through weekly meetings. His suffering brought about a different form of solidarity. Of course, I did what I could to help, but there was little of importance I could actually do. Still, I tried to be with him every step of the way. Like David's relationship with his friend Jonathan, our commitment continued—even after the end of his five-year exhausting battle against the disease. In some real sense, I had become knit to his family, just as David was to Jonathan's.

I say all of this because I want anyone who has endured these pages thus far to understand that **CHESED** is not a theory or a concept but a living, breathing gift of God's nature. Every day that goes by, I realize that I have a myriad number of opportunities to enter into **CHESED** relationships, but only if I am willing. May the good LORD bless each of us with a **CHESED** relationship with the God of the Universe as well as the sweetness and sorrow of true **CHESED** relationships with others.

CHAPTER EIGHT

V'EMETH
(TRUTH)

YHVH YHVH EL RACHUWM V'CHANNUWN EREKH
*APAYIM V'RAV CHESED **V'EMETH**[21]*

The first four characteristics—Compassionate, Gracious, Slow to Anger and Loving-Kindness—are all intimately relational. Our fifth term, **EMETH** *(EMET)*, has important relational qualities as well.

Strong's Lexicon presents **EMETH** as closely connected to our English concepts of stability, certainty, truth, trustworthiness, faithfulness, and sureness. Gesenius's *Hebrew-Chaldee* Lexicon points out that **EMETH**

---

21   Words in reverse order from Hebrew, that is, written from left to right.

describes those who are faithful to their promises—to people, kings and God. Regarding God's judgments, they are trustworthy—entirely **EMETH**:

> *"The fear of the LORD is clean, enduring forever;*
> *The judgments of the LORD are true [**EMETH**];*
> *they are righteous altogether."*
> (Psalm 19:9).

EMETH is a contraction of a Hebrew word that means *"to build up or support; to foster as a parent or nurse; figuratively to render (or be) firm or faithful, to trust or believe, to be permanent or quiet; morally to be true or certain—hence, assurance, believe, bring up, establish, ... be faithful (of long continuance), steadfast, sure, surely, trusty and verified...."* (Strong's H539).

All of that is to say that picking one English word for **EMETH** will not fully catch all of its richness. Plus, we have the word that precedes **CHESED** in the proclamation, our small word **RAV** which means abounding and over-flowing. This means you can either interpret the phrase regarding **EMETH** as being a "standalone," that is, simply Truth as a characteristic, or you can see it as directly tied to the preceding two words as in "abounding in Loving-Kindness AND Truth." The latter reading means that God is saying His "Truth" also abounds and not just His **CHESED**. **RAV**, in that case, would serve to emphasize that God overflows in Truth! Most abundantly! And it is not hard to understand why. God is Truth—the very ground of Truth—He is entirely Trustworthy!

*"Loving-kindness [**CHESED**] and truth [**EMETH**] have met together."* (Psalm 85:10). Here, the Psalmist further emphasizes the special connection between **EMETH** and **CHESED**. Like **RACHUWM** and **CHANNUWN**, they appear frequently as a couplet. They are "joined" relationally, that is, they are wrapped together in meaning. For **CHESED**, this emphasizes that it is REAL—not merely some form of external behavior pattern that one

puts on, but truly faithful, truly not wavering, truly solid in steadfast love. The Hebrew word **PAGASH** connects the two in the Psalm and actually means "join." They are joined together in a deep and penetrating way.

Not only are they joined closely together, the Psalmist reveals that have a unique function for a child of God—the Creator's *"Loving-kindness [CHESED] and Truth [EMETH] will continually **preserve**"* him or her. (Psalm 40:11). Staying in God's Truth and Loving-kindness keeps us from destruction.

The Book of Proverbs further emphasizes their importance. *"Do not let kindness [CHESED] and truth [EMETH] leave you; Bind them around your neck, Write them on the tablet of your heart."* (Proverbs 3:3). Think of what this verse is saying. Both God's Loving-Kindness *[CHESED]* and His Truth *[EMETH]* need to be **bound** tightly on us and written on our **hearts**. Being steadfast in love, totally stable, and also true is not a matter of getting your head straight. It is a matter of the heart. This recalls God's exciting promise through the prophet Jeremiah: *"I will put My law within them and write it on their heart; and I will be their God, and they shall be My people."* (See Jeremiah 31:33 and my *Postscript* after Chapter Twelve).

We could have picked Faithfulness instead of Truth as the primary carrier of meaning for **EMETH**, but I hesitated because **CHESED** itself most clearly embodies the concept of Faithfulness. Another alternative would have been "abounding in Loving-Kindness and **Firmness**," but I hesitated again because surely **CHESED** involves Firmness. A third reading could be "abounding in Loving-Kindness and **Realness**," playing off of the clear "IS-ness" of the Creator: He *IS*! All of these are possible constructions and worth considering because they all speak to God's sureness. Regardless, the certainty that God *IS* entirely as He proclaims to be is good news indeed!

Unfortunately, the last one hundred and sixty years have seen a great shift in the way Western societies think. The slow, steady stain of the philosophical "contributions" of Marx, Hegel, Nietzsche, Sartre, and Foucault has so blemished the cloth of belief that whole societies believe that nothing is real and solid. "Operating Instructions" for much of mankind do not exist. Judeo-Christian certainties about life, death, family, and morals have been thrown out the window.

God's affirmation that He is entirely **EMETH**—entirely real and entirely true—is critical to grasp at this juncture in Western history. What you see is what you get. There is no Mr. Oz in his little jacket masquerading behind the screen. What you see when you see God is Real. What you hear from God is True. We ARE made in the image of God. We matter. We DO have dignity. Life IS important. Actions are important. It all matters. There is no mumbo-jumbo.

In C.S. Lewis's *The Great Divorce*, Lewis pictures the realness of the things of God in the metaphor of concreteness versus ethereal nothingness. Lewis's plot is a delight: a bus trip from Hell to Heaven. A scraggly group of passengers at a bus stop in Hell, whittled down by many arguments, finally board a bus to Heaven. In spite of great complaining along the way, the motley crew lands on the outskirts of Heaven.

The outskirts are wondrous, but complaints continue. Lewis's description of the outskirts is vivid. The narrator, also a passenger from Hell, shares his wonder at the grass and the difference he sees in his companions. They now appear as willowy wraiths, barely visible, while the grass is more real than he could ever have imagined.

Here is the narrator's account:

"At first, … my attention was caught by my fellow-passengers, who were still grouped about in the neighborhood of the omnibus, though beginning, some of them, to walk forward into the landscape with hesitating steps. I gasped when I saw them. Now that they were in the light, they were transparent— fully transparent when they stood between me and it, smudgy and imperfectly opaque when they stood in the shadow of some tree. They were in fact ghosts: man-shaped stains on the brightness of that air. One could attend to them or ignore them at will as you do with the dirt on a windowpane.

"I noticed that the grass did not bend under their feet; even the dew drops were not disturbed. Then some re-adjustment of the mind or some focusing of my eyes took place, and I saw the whole phenomenon the other way round.

"The men were as they had always been; as all the men I had known had been perhaps. It was the light, the grass, the trees that were different; made of some different substance, so much solider than things in our country that men were ghosts by comparison. Moved by a sudden thought, I bent down and tried to pluck a daisy which was growing at my feet. The stalk wouldn't break. I tried to twist it, but it wouldn't twist. I tugged till the sweat stood out on my forehead and I had lost most of the skin off my hands. The little flower was hard, not like wood or even like iron, but like diamond. There was a leaf—a young tender beech-leaf, lying in the grass beside it. I tried to pick the leaf up: my heart almost cracked with the effort, and I believe I did just raise it."[22]

We have no idea how real "REAL" can be nor how false "FALSE" can be. What we often think is real is just a shadow of reality, and what we think is false may be, in fact, real. The dimension of it, the solidity of it, may entirely escape us.

---

22 From C.S. Lewis's *That Hideous Strength*, Chapter Five.

Thinking about God's reality—His **EMETH**—Maimonides wrote, *"But the Eternal is the true God; that is,* **He alone is real, and nothing else has reality like His reality."**[23] (see Jeremiah 10:10).

God is as real as real can be and entirely trustworthy. May we have eyes to see and ears to hear true reality!

---

23 Emphasis mine.

CHAPTER NINE

נֹצֵר חֶסֶד לַאֲלָפִים

NOTSER CHESED LA'ALAPHIM[24]
(PRESERVING LOVING-KINDNESS
TO THOUSANDS)

*"Know therefore that the LORD your God, He is God, the faithful God, Who keeps His covenant and His faithfulness [**CHESED**] to a thousand **generations [DOWR]** for those who love Him and keep His commandments..."* (Deuteronomy 7:9).

The small three-character Hebrew word transliterated **DOWR** in Deuteronomy 7:9 helps us understand just how long the Creator's **CHESED** lasts. The word means "generation." Instead of interpreting God's declaration to Moses as showing love to thousands of people, we see that

---

24 Words in reverse order from the Hebrew, that is, written from left to right.

Moses most likely understood Him to mean a thousand generations. If we assume a generation encompasses approximately thirty years, then we have a declaration that God's **CHESED** will be extended for roughly *THIRTY THOUSAND* years, that is, at least **three hundred centuries**. We still have a long way to go to get to that point. We can imagine the wonder Moses experienced when our Creator God revealed how long His **CHESED** would last for those bound to Him. But we know from our earlier study that God's **CHESED** lasts FOREVER. Therefore, we can assume that God was speaking to Moses metaphorically to emphasize the point that He will stick with Israel forever.

A CHAIN OF PEOPLE

The LORD's promise to show His loving-kindness (**CHESED**) to generation after generation also spotlights the "chain of kindness"[25] that has come to us not only in the form of Scriptures, but also in the generational chain that passes from one generation to another. None of us living in the 21st century have received what we know of God solely from personal revelation. There is a great chain of individual believers laboring in every generation to pass on that which they have received. Every Jewish parent was conscious of this command:

"Hear, Israel! The Lord is our God, the Lord is one! And you shall love the Lord your God with all your heart and with all your soul and with all your strength. These words, which I am commanding you today, shall be on your heart. And you shall repeat them diligently to your sons and speak of them when you sit in your house, when you walk on the road, when you lie down, and when you get up. You shall also tie them as a sign to your hand, and they shall be as frontlets on your forehead. You shall also write them on the doorposts of your house and on your gates." (Deuteronomy 6:4-9).

---

25   See Paul Tudor Jones's *Chain of Kindness*, August House, 1992.

What we receive from God may come directly or through others, whether living or dead—from parents, elders, friends, strangers, covenant communities—in spite of the fact that some lived long before us. Many left behind their own knowledge and experience. It is a great privilege to be a modern-day recipient—to pass on to our children and grandchildren what we have received.

Mezuzah Holder

This two-inch-long *MEZUSAH* holder is affixed to the doorpost of my home. Inside is an amazingly tiny scroll handwritten in the smallest imaginable Hebrew font. It contains the text, *"Hear, O Israel, the LORD our God, the LORD is One."* It is a great reminder to me, my wife, my children, my grandchildren, and all that enter that we want to love the God of the Universe with all of our heart, soul, and strength and our neighbor as ourselves. Even small actions like posting scripture on a doorpost can pass on a blessing to future generations.

Another simple expression of **CHESED** is planting trees that you will not see grow to maturity. The Talmud tells the story of the sage Honi who saw a man planting a carob tree along the road. Honi stopped and asked, *"How many years will it take for this tree to bear fruit?"* The man answered, *"Seventy years."* Noting the man's age, Honi asked if he expected to see the fruit of the tree that he was planting. The man replied, *"Just as my ancestors planted for me, I too am planting for my descendants."*[26]

*"Solidarity [**CHESED**][27],"* Pope John Paul II wrote in his 1987 encyclical, **On Social Concern**, *"is not a feeling of vague compassion or shallow distress at the misfortunes of so many people, both near and far. On the contrary, it is a firm and persevering determination to commit oneself to … the good of all and to each individual…."*[28] Even to those far off—even to those not yet alive.

Know that the Creator of the Universe's **CHESED** has always been operative, is operative, and always will be operative! May our own Steadfast Love, our Loving-Kindness, be constant, never failing, and give real support to those alongside and those to come.

26 The story is taken from the Koren Noe Talmud, 23a.

27 My interpretation.

28 John Paul II, *On Social Concern* [Sollicitudo rei Socialis], no. 38.

CHAPTER TEN

נֹשֵׂא עָוֹן וָפֶשַׁע וְחַטָּאָה

NOSEI AVON VA-PESHA V'CHATTA'AH[29] (FORGIVING INIQUITY, REBELLION, AND SIN)

If you have been surprised at the LORD's proclamation thus far, hold on to your hat. Personally, I find this section astounding. The God of the Universe, just disobeyed by an act of great iniquity (the Golden Calf episode), is proclaiming that He can forgive *(NOSEI)* three types of hurtful human behavior, including the type He has just witnessed. In many English translations, the phrase is *"Forgiving iniquity, rebellion, and sin."* This comment is entirely relational. Think about your closest relationships. How does the bad behavior of close friends affect you? Can you forgive a deep hurt from someone you love—from someone close to you? Or from someone you don't even know?

---

29 Words in reverse order from Hebrew, that is, written from left to right.

My biggest challenge has always been in forgiving those closest to me, including myself. My anger heightened when an infraction involved one of my children or my spouse. What especially pushed me over the edge was when one of the children hurt a brother or a sister. Or when they spoke disrespectfully to their mother. And then there were times when one of them was mistreated by a teacher, coach or other adult. Being able to forgive relational infractions is not easy, but it is a critical component for staying in long-lasting relationships—particularly within a family.

Thus, it is wonderful, fabulous, and fantastic news that the Creator of the Universe CAN forgive. Not only that, it is His "way." He wants to stay close to each one of us—even to the point of forgiving bad actions.

Our three words, **AVON** (aw-VOHN), **PESHA**, and **CHATTA'AH**, occur frequently in what could be called Hebrew Parallels. Most frequently, two are in the form of a couplet. For instance, when the brothers of Joseph ask him for forgiveness, it is for their **PESHA** and their **CHATTA'AH**—their trespasses and their sins—when they abandoned him years earlier, leaving him in a pit out in the desert. (Genesis 50:17). When Aaron sacramentally lays his hands on the head of a live goat on Yom Kippur, it is to lay on the goat all of the **AVON, PESHA**, and **CHATTA'AH** of the Israelites that the Israelites may have their burden lifted. (Leviticus 16:21). All three words are closely associated in meaning, but each has a different emphasis.

Let's look more deeply at each word:

FORGIVING

The first Hebrew word in this section is **NOSEI,** which means "to lift, lift off or carry away." Our English word "forgiving" is a pretty good translation of the Hebrew word even though it misses the sense of lightening the burden of guilt carried by an infractor. It does, however, get to the main point. Just the *willingness* of the Creator of the Universe to forgive anything is remarkable. Certainly, He has no pressure to forgive other than from His own nature. Remember Irenaeus's rather constant refrain in *Against Heresies, "He needs nothing,"* and Maimonides's concurrence that we recalled in Chapter Six.

To forgive is truly an act of Kindness and Mercy, and we are right to recognize that it is often activated by Compassion. Plus, *"Slowness to Anger"* certainly facilitates God's inclination to forgive. In forgiveness, we see aspects of **RACHUWM, CHANNUWN, EREKH APAHIM,** and **CHESED** coming together. They fuel God's forgiveness when we repent for having gotten off track and having done hurtful things to either ourselves, those around us, or those far off.

Of these four enabling characteristics,[30] two stand out as preeminent. Remember King David's great sin with Bathsheba. David calls out to God,

> "*Be gracious [CHANAN] to me, O God,*
> *according to Your loving-kindness [CHESED],*
> *According to the greatness [RAV] of Your compassion [RACHAM], blot out*
> *my transgressions [PESHA].*
> *Wash me thoroughly from my iniquity [AVON]*
> *And cleanse me from my sin [CHATTA'AH].*
> *For I know my transgressions [PESHA],*
> *And my sin [CHATTA'AH] is ever before me."*
> (Psalm 51:1-3).

God's Steadfast Love *[CHESED]* and Compassion *[RACHUWM]* fuel God's willingness to forgive **AVON, PESHA,** and **CHATTA'AH.**

AVON – INIQUITY, PERVERSITY, DEPRAVITY

AVON, our word translated as "iniquity." is the biggest surprise in the list of three malefactions. It is hard to imagine that anyone could forgive **AVON,** a word that can mean perversity and depravity as well as iniquity. These possible translations bring to mind unthinkable human actions. The word **AVON** derives from its root word **AVAH,** which means *bent, twisted, crooked,* or *distorted.*

The word **AVON** is used in Genesis 19:15 to characterize one of the most twisted and bent towns in Biblical history, the town of Sodom. Nearly all who lived there were wicked and perverse. The horrid story of Abraham's nephew, Lot, and the encounter between the people of Sodom and the two messengers sent by God to rescue Lot and his family is graphically recorded in the nineteenth chapter of Genesis. The men of the town wanted

---

30 RACHUWM, CHANNUWN, EREKH APAHIM, CHESED

to commit carnal perversion and violence against Lot's guests. From my point of view, the two guests were **QODESH**—belonging entirely to God— and the iniquity of the townsfolk triggered hail and brimstone falling upon the town.

Another example of **AVON** occurs when an Israelite named Achan commits numerous iniquities during the battle of Jericho as recorded in the Book of Joshua, Chapter 7. Here, instead of sexual perversion, the spotlight is on five criminal actions: unfaithfulness (direct disobedience to a ban on taking objects of value during the battle), stealing, taking for oneself that which is God's (something **QODESH**), deception, and lying. Achan's **AVON**, his "bentness," is revealed in all five.

When we read of such examples—the perverseness of Sodom and the crimes of Achan—it is tempting to stay emotionally on the surface of the story and not catch the depth of the darkness, the bestiality of the bentness, the pungent odor of death and decay that are viscerally perceived. **AVON** is a horror—a toxicity—the exact opposite of the way things should be. Like a serpent's bite, its poison spreads until life is extinguished.

As a young man, I was deeply impacted by the first volume in C.S. Lewis's marvelous space trilogy. Ransom, the hero of ***Out of the Silent Planet***, is captured by two evil men and taken to Mars. There, Ransom breaks free and receives kindness and hospitality from a Martian creature, an *hyossa*.

As Ransom tries to learn the language of the *hyossa*, he discovers the closest English equivalent for describing his earthly captors: the word **bent**. Suddenly his newfound friend, Hyoi, is shot from afar by one of the men who had kidnapped Ransom. Horrified, Ransom exclaims in their dialect, *"Hyoi, it is through me that this has happened. It is the other hmana [humans] who have hit you, the **bent** two that brought me to [your planet]. They can throw death at a distance with a thing they have made.... We* *[humans] are all a **bent** race....' His speech died away into the inarticulate, he did not know the words for forgive, or shame, or fault, hardly the word for sorry. He could only stare into Hyoi's distorted face in speechless guilt."*

Bent! Lewis spotlights the plight of humankind after the Fall in the Garden of Eden. He saw that mankind had become horribly bent and twisted from the shape God intended. I feel sure Lewis was well aware of *AVON's* meaning.

Looking at all the occurrences of the word *AVON* in the Hebrew Bible (over two hundred times), we find that the word is used most frequently to describe sickening, bent, and twisted offenses toward God as well as offenses against things or people dedicated to Him.

PESHA – REBELLION

PESHA is our second type of hurtful act. It is amazing that God can forgive *PESHA*. Its root word, *PASHA*, means to "break away," thus "to rebel." *PESHA* means to go beyond the bounds, whether of authority, relational integrity, or covenant. Though often translated by the English words "transgression" and "trespass," Rabbi A.J. Rosenberg uses the term, *"rebellion"* for *PESHA* in his translation of Exodus 34:7. It is more to the point. Rebellion is certainly "going beyond the bounds."

But *PESHA* is more than going "off track," even though the English words "transgression" and "trespass" have that sense. "Transgression" comes from the Latin *transgressio* which itself derives by combining *trans* (beyond, on the farther side of) and *gressio* (step), thus "going **beyond** the step," that is, "**beyond** the track." Our English word "trespass" is quite similar: "tres" meaning "across" and "pass" from *passus* meaning step or pace, so, "crossing beyond the path." But *PESHA* is more than going "off track" or "crossing beyond the path." It spotlights the **willfulness** to go beyond the path—to rebel—its defining feature.

My sweet wife often points out that I carry around a hidden tendency to **PESHA**, and I confess she is right. After forty-seven years of NOT repenting of it, I am doing my best to repent. I typically think I have a justification for my behavior, but so does every other rebellious spirit. My self-justification doesn't trump my willfulness. While driving, I would come to a poorly engineered signal light that was not programmed to take into account that there were no other cars in sight from any direction. If the signal light was red for more than forty seconds, I would willfully run the red light and feel entirely justified in doing so. I *felt* entirely justified—that is, until I sat with Exodus 34:7 and this word, **PESHA**. It was then that I realized there was a willfulness tinged with pride that had fueled my "stepping beyond the bounds."

Worse for all of us, however, may be the tendency to **PESHA** by speaking speak ill of those in authority over us. Our political elections in the United States set a record for rancor and defamation. Going beyond the bounds of authority can begin with just one deprecating word. This is what happened with King David's third son, Absalom (*Abiyshalowm* in Hebrew). 2nd Samuel (**SHMUEL**) 15:6 says, *"Absalom stole away the hearts of the men of Israel"* with critical comments about his father. It wasn't long before Absalom was leading an outright revolt. Many were hurt terribly, not only King David but also followers on both sides. Eventually, Absalom suffered a terrible tragedy that linked back to his underlying pride.

All of us are positioned within realms of authority, whether they be within the realm of God's authority or within the realms of federal, state, municipal, organizational (think work, school, church, non-profit), or family authority. The spirit of **PESHA** is NOT limited to a Biblical geography; we can find it alive and well in our family home.

CHATTA'AH – SIN

CHATTA'AH is the Hebrew word we most often encounter translated as *"sin."* I grew up thinking every infraction was a sin. The distinctions behind **PESHA** and **AVON** were beyond me. In my mind, everything was just "missing the mark." The idea of a willingness to "go beyond the path" or of being truly "bent and twisted" was hidden within a broad idea of sin. As a younger man, I wish that I had known more about God, more about myself, and more about the richness of Biblical language.

The Hebrew word, **CHATTA'AH** (pronounced Hah-Ta-AHH with a strong guttural on the first syllable), comes from the root word **CHATA** which means "miss the path," "miss the mark," or "wander from the path." We can see immediately that the root word is somewhat related in meaning to **PESHA**, that is, "going beyond the path." But the root is different in a subtle way—more like making an unintentional but hurtful mistake.

My earliest introduction to the concept behind **CHATTA'AH** was at least fifty years ago, when someone explained that sin was like missing the bull-seye on an archery or rifle target. That made sense to me. If we are "off the mark," we are somewhere that we should not be.

Robin Hood by Parker Weber, age 10

In Biblical usage, being "off the mark" occurs every time we do what we shouldn't do. Relationally, there are a myriad number of ways that we can be off the mark, and the same is true in our relation to Holy things—things that are **QODESH**, wholly devoted to God.

Like Robin Hood, we all hope to hit the relational bull's eye, but truthfully, who amongst us is as good as that legendary marksman! All of us miss the mark, and some miss continuously. There is a long list of **CHATTA'AH** occurrences called out in the Hebrew Scriptures. My Jewish friends count six-hundred and thirteen **MITZVOT** (commandments) that we can disobey or fail to observe. Each violated **MITZVAH** misses the mark and thus would be **CHATTA'AH**—though various ones also would be **AVON** or **PESHA**.

Jesus of Nazareth summed up the most important **MITZVAH**: "*'You shall love the Lord your God with all your heart, and with all your soul, and with all your mind.' This is the great and foremost commandment. The second is like it, 'You shall love your neighbor as yourself.' Upon these two commandments hang the whole Law and the Prophets.*" (Matthew 22:36-40).

Rabbi Jonathan Sachs condensed the **MITZVOT** in a more expansive way: "*Love your neighbour. Love the stranger. Hear the cry of the otherwise unheard. Liberate the poor from their poverty. Care for the dignity of all. Let those who have more than they need share their blessings with those that have less. Feed the hungry, house the homeless, and heal the sick in body and mind. Fight injustice, whoever it is done by and whoever it is done against. And do these things because, being human, we are bound by a covenant of human solidarity, whatever our colour or culture, class or creed. These are moral principles, not economic or political ones. They have to do with conscience, not wealth or power. But without them, freedom will not survive.*"[31]

---

31   Rabbi Jonathan Sachs, *Morality* (New York, Hachette Books, 2020), x.

Six-hundred and thirteen commandments are a lot, though in our day, my Jewish friends have fewer to worry about since the temple no longer functions, and many of the *MITZVOT* were directly related to Temple ritual regulations.

The Book of Leviticus is full of ritual procedures for lifting or covering an offense from God's point of view. But even with ritual procedures, God's forgiveness does not remove all the consequences of sin. Think of the horrid story of King David and Bathsheba, the wife of Uriah. David takes Bathsheba in lust and has her husband, Uriah, killed. To some degree, our Creator lifts the punishment David was due, yet not only is Uriah entirely dead, but the offspring of David's illicit union also dies. God partially lifts David's punishment, but He does not raise Uriah and the baby back to life.

Breaking covenant is another serious example of *CHATTA'AH*. Divorce frequently occurs in spite of the fact that vows were taken to remain together *"until death do us part."* God *CAN* forgive the sin of dividing what is bound, but the impact on children and grandchildren will be felt for generations. This thought will be expanded when we discuss the last section of Exodus 34:7.

Nearly a thousand years ago, Maimonides felt that human forgiveness could be carried out on three levels:

Level One: *"When one person sins against another, he becomes liable for the consequences of the sin that he committed. In order to be relieved of any punishment, he must appease both God and the person that he sinned against. If the person sinned against forgives the perpetrator of his act, the forgiving person relieves the perpetrator of any Heavenly punishment."*

Level Two: *"A higher level of forgiveness is to forgive not just the act of sin, but the sinner himself, even though one person may forgive another for a* *particular bad act (thus relieving him from being punished), there still may remain a trace of dislike for the person in general. Thus, a higher level of forgiveness is to forgive the entire person completely for his wrong, so that there remains no trace of bad feeling between them."*

Level Three: *"The highest level of forgiveness is an emotion that is so strong and positive that it actually uproots the sins of the past, making it as if they never occurred at all (cf. Yoma 86a). After such a forgiveness, the sinner will be loved by the offended party to the very same degree that he was loved before the sin."[32]*

For us, on the receiving end of God's willingness to forgive, is our need for repentance—*TESHUVAH* in Hebrew. *"When a man or woman commits one of the sins of humanity, transgressing against God, the soul bears guilt; they must confess the sin they committed."* (Numbers 5:6-7). And *"he will confess regarding that which he sinned."* (Leviticus 5:5).

Confessing one's sin and repenting from the heart puts us in a spot to receive God's merciful forgiveness. Real repentance carries with it the radical resolution to turn from one's wicked ways—completely. *TESHUVAH* means "returning." When I think of the word *return*, I think of Jesus's marvelous Parable of the Prodigal Son. In that sense, *TESHUVAH* is *returning to the Father's house.* Turning from one's wicked ways is good; going back to Father's house is even better! May it be so for each of us!

SUMMARY

The Creator's willingness to forgive iniquity, transgression and sin is certainly good news. The bad news is that we are all "bent" to some degree; that is, we are all susceptible to perversion. We willfully go beyond the bounds

---

32 Paraphrased from Chaim Miller's reflection on "Forgiveness from Moshe."
https://www.chabad.org/parshah/article_cdo/aid/680266/jewish/Learning-the-Art-of-Forgiveness-from-Moshe.htm

and hit the target far from the bull's eye of perfection in both our attitudes and actions. God has given us clearly written words—*His Operating Instructions for Humankind*—in Scripture. We do well to heed His word.

But the bigger issue is that going our way as opposed to God's way has serious repercussions. We desperately should want to be doing the right thing out of a Godly nature. After all, He made us in His image, and we should want to reflect it. Out of love, He wants His creation to be beautifully whole, without stain or wrinkle.

AVON, *PESHA*, and *CHATTA'AH* are hurtful blemishes. My recommendation? First, pay attention to God's Operating Instructions! You will avoid much trouble!

"The Law of the Lord is perfect, restoring the soul; The testimony of the Lord is sure, making wise the simple. The precepts of the Lord are right, rejoicing the heart; The commandment of the Lord is pure, enlightening the eyes. The fear of the Lord is clean, enduring forever; The judgments of the Lord are true; they are righteous altogether. They are more desirable than gold, yes, than much pure gold; Sweeter also than honey and drippings of the honeycomb. Moreover, Your servant is warned by them; In keeping them there is great reward." (Psalm 19:7-11).

Second, truly repent of what is out of order in your life, dedicate yourself ENTIRELY to God, allow yourself to be *QODESH*—wholly devoted to Him—and pray for His indwelling presence. Then watch for His Mercy and Grace to be with you in a wondrous way!

CHAPTER ELEVEN

וְנַקֵּה לֹא יְנַקֶּה פֹּקֵד עֲוֹן אָבוֹת עַל־
בָּנִים וְעַל־בְּנֵי בָנִים עַל־שִׁלֵּשִׁים
וְעַל־רִבֵּעִים

V'NAQEI LO Y'NAQEI POQED AVON
AVOT AL-BANIM V'AL-BANEI VANIM
AL-SHILLESHIM V'AL-RIBE'IM[33]

(YET HE DOES NOT COMPLETELY CLEAR
[OF SIN]. HE VISITS THE INIQUITY OF
PARENTS ON THE CHILDREN AND ON
THE CHILDREN'S CHILDREN, TO THE THIRD
AND FOURTH GENERATIONS)

---

33 Words in reverse order from Hebrew, i.e., written from left to right.

There has been a great deal of good news since the Creator of the Universe began to speak to Moses in the cleft of the rock—at least, until we get to this very last section. Let's look closer.

Broadly, our translation of this last section assures us that the guilty will not go unpunished. What is this: a switcheroo? First, God says that he forgives iniquity, rebellion, and sins and then He says that He doesn't completely clear the guilty. So, how does that work?

If you are ten years old and you give one of my children a black eye on the playground, what happens if I truly forgive you? It means that **I will not hold that hurt or infraction against you**—neither now nor in the future, neither emotionally nor practically. In an emotional sense, I wipe clean my initial judgment of your action. Though you hurt one of mine, we will be on a clean slate in our future dealings, emotionally and practically.

Maimonides emphasized this: *"A person should be easily placated and difficult to anger, and when the sinner asks him for forgiveness, he should forgive him with a full heart and a willing spirit."* It is not hard to imagine that our own forgiving should mimic that of the Almighty, that is, with a full heart and a willing spirit. But that is easier said than done.

Suppose the black eye you gave my child damages his or her eyesight. Will my extension of forgiveness wipe away the damage? No, it will remain until fully healed. If it doesn't fully heal, it may remain the rest of my child's life.

My wife had a younger brother whose name was Bart. When he was ten years old, little Bart was shot in the face with a small derringer while playing with a neighborhood boy of the same age. The boy's father had hidden the gun in his chest of drawers, never imagining that the boys would find it. Tragically, the gun was loaded, and little Bart died almost instantly. Needless to say, both sets of parents were devastated.

Of course, both the ten-year-old boy who shot Bart and the boy's father were immensely sorry. But Fran's parents had already lost one child in an automobile accident two year earlier, so the loss for them was immeasurable. Yet, they forgave the family as best they could and prayed for their emotional recovery. All the same, little Bart was gone.

The loss of little Bart continues to this day. Our children did not enjoy his potential antics as a doting uncle, nor those of their cousins who might have been born had Bart married years later. God has so fashioned our existence that the consequences of our actions remain with us as vivid reminders, good and bad.

Before we focus on several phrases in the ending section of Exodus 34:7, let's look first at the entire sequence in transliterated Hebrew (reading from left to right):

**"V'NAQEI LO Y'NAQEI POQED AVON AVOT
AL-BANIM V'AL-BANEI VANIM AL-SHILLESHIM
V'AL-RIBE'IM."** (Exodus 34:7b)

And then as translated in the Modern English Translation:

*"Yet He does not completely clear [of sin].
He visits the iniquity of parents on the children and on the
children's children, to the third and fourth generations."*

Now, let's break this up in smaller bites.

V'NAQEI LO Y'NAQEI

NAQEI appears twice in succession separated by *LO* which means "no." Normally, one *NAQEI* would mean "clear, clean, or free from punishment or consequences." We would all like to be clear, clean and free from consequences, but when the word **LO** appears between two **NAQEI**'s, it can be interpreted as "clearing but not completely." Instead of being clear of consequences, it means being subject to consequences. In other words, it means God does *NOT* clear away the consequences. As in the case of the derringer and little Bart, there are consequences for our actions, and they continue long after.

In bold, the New International Translation renders **V'NAQEI LO Y'NAQEI** as "*But He **does not leave** the guilty **unpunished**...*" (NIV).

Compare this with the Jewish Publication Society version: "*that will **by no means clear** the guilty...*" (JPS *Tanakh* 1917)

And the King James: "***by no means clearing** the guilty...*"

And Young's: "***not entirely acquitting...***"

In essence, **V'NAQEI LO Y'NAQEI** simply means "not clearing" or "not entirely clearing."

POQED AVON AVOT

POQED is the Hebrew verb frequently translated as "to visit" or "to punish."

"***visiting** the iniquity of the fathers upon the children, and upon the children's children, unto the third and unto the fourth generation.*" (JPS *Tanakh* 1917).

"***visiting** the iniquity of fathers on the children and on the grandchildren to the third and fourth generations.*" (NASB).

But the word **POQED** also can mean "paying attention" and "watching over." Since the next two words in the sequence are our word for iniquity, **AVON,** and the word **AVOT** which means "fathers," the phrase could be rendered "*watching over the iniquity of the fathers*" or "*paying attention to* *the iniquity of the fathers."* This is a considerable shift in meaning from many translations and perhaps more to the point. *The Living Torah* as translated by Rabbi Aryeh Kaplan is one of the few translations that renders this section with a similar understanding:

"... He does not clear [those who do not repent] but keeps in mind the sins of the fathers to their children and grandchildren, to the third and fourth generation."

We need to remember that we are talking here about the Creator of the Universe and His "ways." Whether He *"visits"* the iniquity of the fathers, or *"pays attention to"* the iniquity of the fathers, or *"keeps in mind"* the iniquity of the fathers, I do not know for certain. But what is certain is that **consequences have consequences**—a father's *AVON* (iniquity or bentness) has effects beyond the father's generation. Without question, this is *EMETH*, true truth.

No matter how hidden or how overt, the iniquity, perverseness, twistedness, and bentness of any father or mother has repercussions on their children and the children's children. The most important takeaway is that ungodliness has repercussions, and the more ungodly the behavior, the greater the repercussions on future generations.

V'AL-BANEI VANIM AL-SHILLESHIM V'AL-RIBE'IM

BANIM is the Hebrew word for sons or children. When repeated, we have the "children's children." *SHILLESHIM* means "third generation," and *RIBE'IM* means "fourth generation." Put together, we have *"upon the children, and upon the children's children, unto the third and unto the fourth generation."* (JPS *Tanakh* 1917). Consequences of our *AVON* extend far beyond our generation.

SUMMING UP

We are at the end of our two verses. The God of the Universe has answered Moses's plea; God's "ways" have been declared. Wonderful news overall, but the sober ending reminds us that our hurtful actions, even when forgiven, can have a negative effect long after we are gone. In spite of the appalling iniquity of the Golden Calf infraction, Moses next hears God reaffirm His covenantal intentions to remain faithful to the rebellious Israelites. The LORD of the Universe reaffirms His covenant. We serve a marvelous Creator!

CHAPTER TWELVE

SPARK SOME KINDNESS

In November of 2019, Walmart released **Spark Some Kindness**, an *a capella* video for the holiday season. My son Russell co-wrote the lyrics, and for me, those lyrics highlight one of the main things that comes to us from our Creator—loving-kindness. If you substitute **CHESED** for Love and Kindness, you'll get the picture.

> *It's about the giving and sharing of Love...*
> *If we can spark some Kindness* [**CHESED**] *in the World*
> *From the bottom of our Hearts,*
> *It wouldn't be so Dark,*
> *If we could learn to Love one another*
> *That would be a start.*
> *So Open Up, Buckle Up,...*
> *It's time for us to do our part.*

The nature of God and His ways are meant to be OUR nature and OUR ways. Religious language can obscure the good news. Where God is, Kindness is! And He wants to light up the world with *OUR* Kindness! That is super news!

Remember in the first chapter that we said we can't really answer "Who we are?" until we can answer, "Who is God?" Bottomline, we've learned from Exodus 34:6-7 that our Creator is all about a loving-kindness that is shown in a multitude of ways. He is compassionate, gracious, slow to anger, abounding in steadfast love and truth, showing steadfast love to thousands of generations, forgiving iniquity, rebellion, and sin while allowing the constraint of consequences to help us keep from blemishing the beauty of life in God for future generations.

WE SHOULD BE LIKE HIM

Verses 6 and 7 of the 34th Chapter of Exodus stand as two of the most important verses in Scripture. The more we contemplate the ways of the LORD, the deeper we go. The Creator is entirely **QODESH** (HOLY), and we should be like Him.

Rabbi Jonathan Sacks used portions of Exodus 34:6-7 as well as encouragements from Maimonides' nine-hundred-year-old texts to call everyone to be like the Lord of the Universe:

*"One of the most striking propositions of the Torah is that **we are called on, as God's image, to imitate God**. "Be Holy, for I, the Lord your God, am Holy" (Leviticus 19:2). The sages taught: "Just as God is called gracious [**RACHUWM**], so you be gracious [**RACHUWM**]. Just as He is called merciful [**V'CHANNUWN**], so you be merciful [**V'CHANNUWN**]. Just as He is called holy [**QODESH**], so you be holy [**QODESH**]." So too the prophets described the Almighty by all the various attributes: long-suffering [**EREKH***

*APAYIM], abounding in kindness [**RAV CHESED**], righteous, upright, per-*
fect, mighty, and powerful and so on—to teach us that these qualities are
*good and right and that a human being should cultivate them, and thus **imi-***
***tate God as far as we can**."*[34]

"*Imitate God as far as we can!*" This is easier said than done.

"*It is known and certain that the love of God does not become closely knit in*
a man's heart till he is continuously and thoroughly possessed by it and gives
up everything else in the world for it; as God commanded us, with all your
heart and with all your soul...."[35]

Both Jews and Christians believe that we are to be like Him! Teaching a
large crowd on the side of a hill in Galilee, Jesus emphasized "*Therefore, be*
perfect, as your heavenly Father is perfect."[36]

My Jewish friends emphasize a life that takes "*diligent heed to do the com-*
mandment and the law, which Moses the servant of the LORD charged you,
to love the LORD your God, and to walk in all His ways, and to keep His
commandments, and to cleave unto Him, and to serve Him with all your
***heart and with all your soul.*"** (Joshua 22:5; emphasis mine).

Christians emphasize the necessity of coming to God though a deep,
life-changing repentance—giving oneself over entirely to the lordship
of God as Father, Jesus as son, and by receiving the gift of the **RUACH**
ADONAI, the Spirit of God, to illuminate their way and direct their path.

---

34 Rabbi Jonathan Sacks reflection referencing Rabbi Moshe ben Maimon's
("Maimonides") *Mishneh Torah*, Sefer Madda, Hilcot De'ot, Chapter One, sections 5-6.,
rabbisacks.org., 2018.10.03. [my emphases].

35 Maimonides on the Love of God from Mishneh Torah, Book 1, Laws of Repentance,
Chapter X.

36 NIV.

All celebrate the wonder of God's deliverance of His people from Egypt and His great proclamation on Mount Sinai. My prayer is that we all will truly walk in the ways of God. May we often say, "LORD, You are compassionate, gracious, slow to anger, abounding in steadfast love and truth, showing steadfast love to thousands of generations. You can even forgive iniquity, rebellion and sin. Let me follow Your ways and avoid bad consequences for myself and others!"

Let's end this excursion into the Ways of God with two Scriptures that are basically two prayers:

> *"Make me know Your ways, LORD;*
> *Teach me Your paths.*
> *Lead me in Your truth and teach me,*
> *For You are the God of my salvation;*
> *For You I wait all the day."*
> (Psalm 25:4-5).

"I pray that the eyes of your heart may be enlightened, so that you will know what is the hope of His calling, what are the riches of the glory of His inheritance in the saints...." (Ephesians 1:18).

POSTSCRIPT
FROM A CHRISTIAN POINT OF VIEW

"Now unto the King Eternal,
immortal, invisible, the only God,
be honor and glory
forever and ever.
Amen."
(Paul's 1st letter to Timothy, 1:17)

The proclamation of the Creator of the Universe to His servant Moses is a key point in human history as well as the history of God's Chosen People. Along with the LORD's concrete actions, His direct recorded words help us grasp a sense of just Who He is. This revelation is as important to Christians as it is to Abraham's direct bloodline.

EVERY WORD

Certainly, every word that came through the Prophets of old at the instigation of the Almighty should be precious to every living soul. And what could be more precious than words that came directly from the physical presence of the Almighty Himself?

Recorded instances of God's voice being heard directly are few indeed. Exodus 34:6-7 is on a pinnacle with only a few other verses in all of Scripture that record the direct external voice of God. This doesn't mean we think God has a "mouth" as we think of human anatomy, but clearly Moses *heard* God's proclamation on the Mount. There are other instances recorded in the Book of Genesis and Exodus of direct encounters—Adam and Eve, Cain, Enoch, Noah, Abraham, Isaac, Rebekah, Jacob, Moses, Aaron, and Miriam—but it is not always clear how those messages were delivered.

We also encounter prophetic messages that were revealed to priests, prophets, kings, and holy men and women after the Exodus period, but in many of those instances, they were transmitted through the *apprehension* of a divine message by some other means than that of actually *hearing* audible words. Some of these messages were written by human writers transcribing what they *felt* God was "speaking"—prophetic writing so to speak. No matter how they came, the messages were clear, precise, and extremely pertinent. They needed to be since the messages were released to the people for whom they were written as *"The Word of the LORD."* That said, the non-audible "words" are in a different category from what Moses encountered on the Mount. My earlier book, *Visions, Dreams and Encounters*, spotlights some of the non-audible occurrences.

My Jewish friends believe canonical Scriptural revelation ceased before the Common Era. Christians, on the other hand, believe that God's revelation from a canonical point of view did not cease until around the end of 1st Century. These additional Scriptures are frequently called the *"New Testament"* in reference to the new covenant that the Prophet Jeremiah specifically prophesied would come to pass. In my view, the additional verses are a seamless continuation of the prophetic utterances contained in the *Tanakh*. Christians believe Jeremiah's "New Covenant" was ushered in at Jesus's death in exact accord with Jeremiah's prophecy:

*"'Behold, days are coming,' declares the Lord, 'when I will make a **new covenant** with the house of Israel and the house of Judah, not like the covenant which I made with their fathers on the day I took them by the hand to bring them out of the land of Egypt, My covenant which they broke, although I was a husband to them,' declares the Lord. 'For this is the covenant which I will make with the house of Israel after those days,' declares the Lord: 'I will put My law within them and write it on their heart; and I will be their God, and they shall be My people. They will not teach again, each one his neighbor and each one his brother, saying, "Know the Lord," for they will all know Me, from the least of them to the greatest of them,' declares the Lord, 'for I will forgive their wrongdoing, and their sin I will no longer remember.'"* (Jeremiah 31: 31-34).*

A WILD OLIVE SHOOT

Christians of non-Jewish descent believe that they have been grafted into the tree of Israel like a wild olive shoot and therefore partake of the richness and fatness of its root. (Romans 11:17). We consider ourselves part of Abraham's family. Unfortunately, we have plenty of reasons to be ashamed of our historical behavior; often we have acted more like estranged relatives, feuding frequently with our kinfolk, often with tragic results.

My hope in this postscript is to reflect briefly on the similar ways in which most Jews and Christians view the Creator and how these views fit into the boundaries of God's ways as evidenced in Exodus 34:6-7.

Both groups believe wholeheartedly that God is One. No doubt, this may come as a surprise to many of my Jewish friends. From a distance it appears that Christians believe in two Gods, that is, God the Father and Jesus.

But as Chapter Three (*The Name*) hints, the Hebrew reference to God as **ELOHIYM** suggests to Christians that the unity of the One True God is expressed in the Christian concept of tri-unity, that is, three in One: Father, Son and Holy Spirit.

Maimonides was quite adamant that the Oneness and Unity of God made it absolutely impossible to accept the notion expounded in the Trinity. Part of his belief arose from thinking of a God Who has no attributes—Who could *not* have attributes. Maimonides was careful to focus on the LORD's "*ways*" as proclaimed on Mount Sinai rather than on His *nature*. In his **Guide for the Perplexed**, Maimonides stated that *"God has no essential attribute in any form or in any sense whatever, and that the rejection of corporeality implies the rejection of essential attributes. Those who believe that God is One, and that He has many attributes declare the unity with their lips and assume plurality in their thoughts. This is like the doctrine of the Christians, who say that He is one and He is three, and that the three are one."* (**Guide for the Perplexed**, Chapter 51).

My counter thinking goes back to the formation of belief. For all of us, the way we perceive and grasp reality rests to a great degree on what we have seen, read, or experienced—or upon that which we believe others have experienced. Thus, from one point of view, it makes total sense to conceive of God as Maimonides did—based on his exhaustive readings in the **TORAH** and the *Tanakh*—much of which, of course, was straight prophesy. Plus, Maimonides was a master of the **Talmud**, the massive Jewish commentary on the Holy Writings. But for Christians who accept what was recorded of Jesus's ministry by eyewitnesses in the First Century—what many different people testified and experienced through specific prophetic voices and miracles similar to those recorded in the Hebrew Scriptures—an entirely different dimension has entered their field of vision. Their understanding has to fit the facts that they believe are true.

I will not belabor this point; both Jews and Christians still say with assurance, *The LORD ELOHIYM is One LORD!* (Deuteronomy 6:4).

Both groups also believe that the LORD is entirely *Other*. Both groups believe that He has revealed Himself to mankind through His presence, His miracles (interventions in the created realm), His prophets, and through Scripture. It is in the identification of the true prophets and miracles that we run into difficulty. The extensive prophetic voices recorded in "New Testament" Scriptures include those of the angel Gabriel, the prophetess Anna, Mary (mother of Jesus), Zacharias the Levite, Elizabeth (wife of Zacharias), John the Baptist, Simeon, the Apostles Peter, John (brother of James), Paul, Philip's daughters, Agabus, and a host of others, including Jesus himself.

These prophetic voices testified to a truly earth-shaking event—God entering into humanity as a sacrificial offering that would atone for sin as well as usher in the New Covenant Jeremiah had prophesied. Undoubtedly, this Messianic event required an adjustment in the minds of those who loved God as they had come to know Him—those who had a great love for His Word and Scripture.

Christians believe that Jesus was anointed with the **RUACH QODESH** (Holy Spirit). Jesus's earthly ministry was identified so closely with his prophetic anointing that his name was soon tagged in Greek as *"CHRISTOS,"* which simply means *the Anointed One*—in Hebrew, the **MASHIYACH**—in English, the *Messiah*. Additionally, the Christian New Testament Scriptures are peppered with angelic visitations, miracles, and at least two direct God-proclamations during Jesus's earthly ministry. God's audible proclamations are recorded at Jesus's baptism and on what Christians call the Mount of Transfiguration. My Jewish friends do not recognize any of these occurrences as legitimate.

Christians believe that the birth of Jesus and his later actions fulfilled many of God's promises articulated earlier by Jewish prophets. In other words, Christians believe that the narrative of Jesus flows seamlessly from the preceding prophetic voices. He is a unique link in the "chain of kindness." But this has been difficult for Orthodox Jewish believers to even consider.

Few of my Jewish friends believe that the "New Covenant" promised by Jeremiah was ushered in by Jesus's death or that Jesus might be the **MASHIYACH**—the long-awaited Messiah. Conversely, Christians believe his very death *WAS* the covenant-making (**KARATH BERIYTH**) moment, that is, the moment when the God of the Universe cut the promised New Covenant with mankind in the death of Jesus himself. Admittedly, all of this spotlights a huge difference in belief.

Jesus's multiple roles add fuel to the fire. He was a preeminent **Teacher** (*Rabbi*) of the masses. He spoke as a **Prophet** and was received as a **King** and **Lord** (**KYRIOS** in Greek and **RABBONI** in Aramaic). He was an astounding **Healer** (ushering in God's healing to the sick, lame, and blind). And at His crucifixion, He served as **Priest** (the Anointed One) and even served as the sacrificial lamb.

Rabbi Sacks has a remarkable passage in his book, *The Book of Redemption (Covenant & Conversation)*, where he sheds light on some of the differences between Priests and Prophets. First, he focuses on the difference in the words that are most frequently uttered by each group. Our Hebrew word for Holy, **QODESH**, and its opposite are the focus of the Priest. The Prophet focuses on **TZEDEK** (Righteousness) and **MISHPAT** (Justice), **CHESED** (Loving-kindness), and **RACHUWM** (Compassion). Rabbi Sacks continues, "*The key verbs of priesthood are ... to instruct and distinguish. The key activity of the Prophet is to proclaim, 'the word of the Lord.'... The priest speaks the word of God for all time; the prophet, the word of God for his time.*" I would add that the Priest *deals* with sacrifices, whereas the

Prophet *calls* for sacrifice. In all these distinctions, Christians see Jesus functioning in both roles. Ultimately, we feel he *is* the sacrifice!

But instead of dwelling on differences, let's look at how similarly the early Christians, including Jesus himself, proclaimed and demonstrated the various acts and attitudes that are articulated in Exodus 34:6-7.

PARABLE OF THE PRODIGAL SON

As an itinerant rabbi, Jesus taught in parables. Jesus's *Parable of the Prodigal Son* reveals the nature of the Creator as a Father **abounding in loving-kindness**—one who also is **slow to anger**, full of **compassion**, and extends undeserved **graciousness**. Jesus's parable tells the story of a father's younger son who had left home and fallen into dissipation. Coming to his senses far from home, the young man said to himself,

*"I will set out and go to my father, and will say to him, 'Father, I have sinned against heaven, and in your sight; I am no longer worthy to be called your son; treat me as one of your hired laborers.' So, he set out and came to his father. But when he was still a long way off, his father saw him and felt **compassion** for him and ran and **embraced** him and **kissed** him. And the son said to him, 'Father, I have sinned against heaven and in your sight; I am no longer worthy to be called your son.' But the father said to his slaves, 'Quickly **bring out the best robe** and put it on him and **put a ring on his finger and sandals on his feet**; and **bring the fattened calf**, slaughter it, and let's eat and celebrate; for this son of mine was dead and has come to life again; he was lost and has been found.'"* (Luke 15:18-24).

In spite of what the young man's behavior might have deserved, we see the heart of the father representing God writ large—**a heart that forgives iniquity, rebellion, and sin, abounds in steadfast love, is slow to anger, and displays amazing compassion and graciousness.**

GOD AS FATHER

In his attempt to paint the Parable of the Prodigal Son, Rembrandt caught much of the father's pathos in his famous painting that now hangs in St. Petersburg's Hermitage Museum:

Jesus's parable emphasizes his penetrating perception of God as Father and particularly God as Father of both Israel and the rest of mankind. God's *Otherness* along with His great power (think of His Exodus display to Israel in fire and thunder) appear to have made the concept of God as an intimate Father hard for the Children of Israel to imagine. The first direct indication that God might be related to as a Father does not occur until the fourth chapter of Exodus. There, God instructs Moses on his task of freeing the Israelites from Egypt. God tells Moses to say to Pharaoh, *"**Israel is my first-born son**, and I told you, 'Let my people go.'"* (Exodus 4:22-23).

Later, Moses hinted at God's fatherly role through metaphors. For example, Moses reproves the Israelites using a metaphor to portray God as Father: *"and in the wilderness where you saw how the LORD your God carried you, just as a man carries his son, in all the way which you have walked until you came to this place. But for all this, you did not trust the LORD your God."* (Deuteronomy 1:31-32).

Eventually, Moses directly emphasized the Creator's familial relationship in Chapter 32 of Deuteronomy: *"Is this what you do to the LORD, you foolish and unwise people?* ***Is He not your Father*** *Who has purchased you? He has made you and established you."* Deuteronomy 32:6).

James Kugel, Starr Professor Emeritus of Hebrew Literature at Harvard University and a specialist in the Hebrew Bible as well as the Dead Sea Scrolls, discerns in his book, ***The Great Shift***, a shift in people's understanding of God and the individual self over the period of time in which the Hebrew Scriptures were composed. In other words, the Children of Israel understood God in different ways depending on the era in which they found themselves.

Since we have only a handful of references to God as *Father* in the Torah, it makes Isaiah's prophecies even more precious. Aside from the Torah and Psalms, it was the Prophet Isaiah that Jesus quoted most in his teachings. Isaiah himself quoted God declaring that those called by His name are His sons and daughters:

> *"Do not fear, for I am with you;*
> *I will bring your offspring from the east,*
> *And gather you from the west.*
> *I will say to the north, 'Give them up!'*
> *And to the south, 'Do not hold them back.'*
> ***Bring My sons from afar***
> ***And My daughters from the ends of the earth,***
> *Everyone who is called by My name,*
> *And whom I have created for My glory,*
> *Whom I have formed, even whom I have made."*
> (Isaiah 43:5-7).

We can detect an even more striking shift by the time we get to the Christian New Testament Scriptures. Not only is Jesus's extraordinarily intimate relationship with God revealed on almost every page, we see him teaching his disciples that they, too, are children of God and meant to live in a deep awareness of that intimacy.

"What person is there among you who, when his son asks for a loaf of bread, will give him a stone? Or if he asks for a fish, he will not give him a snake, will he? So, if you, despite *being evil, know how to give good gifts to your children, how much more will your* **Father Who is in heaven** *give good things to those who ask Him!"* (Matthew 7:9-11).

JESUS'S PRAYER FOR HIS DISCIPLES

One day, several of his disciples asked him how they should pray. Jesus's answer reveals how imbedded the idea of God as Father was to Jesus. The word "Father" appears four times in this very short section on prayer from the Book of Matthew:

"And when you are praying, do not use thoughtless repetition as the Gentiles do, for they think that they will be heard because of their many words. So, do not be like them; for your **Father** *knows what you need before you ask Him:*

'Our **Father,** *Who is in heaven,*
Hallowed be Your name.
Your kingdom come.
Your will be done,
On earth as it is in heaven.
Give us this day our daily bread.
And forgive us our debts,
as we also have forgiven our debtors.

And do not lead us into temptation,
but deliver us from evil.'

For if you forgive other people for their offenses, your
heavenly Father *will also forgive you. But if you do not forgive*
*other people, then your **Father** will not forgive your offenses."*
(Matthew 6:7-15).

PARABLE OF THE GOOD SAMARITAN

In addition to Jesus's emphasis on knowing God as Father, we find him constantly extending *compassion* as well as *graciousness*, particularly to the downtrodden. Since his sayings in the New Testament Scriptures have come down to us via Greek texts, we do not have a totally direct link back to the Hebrew text of Exodus 34:6. But, because of the Septuagint (the Greek translation of the Hebrew Scriptures), we can feel fairly confident that Jesus was referencing the same proclamation words in Exodus 34:6-7 in much of his teaching (probably in their Aramaic equivalent).

God's **Compassion** and **Graciousness** is on direct display in the Parable of the Good Samaritan. The Samaritans were held in contempt by those who worshipped God at the temple in Jerusalem. Jesus's parable focuses on the question, "Who is our neighbor?" But the spotlight that shines on **compassion** and **gracious acts** relates back to God Himself. Though the Samaritan had absolutely no reason aside from his *compassion* to help the Jewish man who has been badly battered by robbers along the way, he extended astounding *graciousness* to the robbers' victim. Here is the setting and the story:

"… [an expert in Mosaic Law] stood up and put [Jesus] to the test, saying, 'Teacher, what shall I do to inherit eternal life?' And He said to him, 'What is written in the Law? How does it read to you?' And he answered, 'You shall

love the Lord your God with all your heart, and with all your soul, and with all your strength, and with all your mind; and your neighbor as yourself.' And He said to him, 'You have answered correctly; do this and you will live.' But wanting to justify himself, he said to Jesus, 'And who is my neighbor?'

"Jesus replied and said, 'A man was going down from Jerusalem to Jericho, and he encountered robbers, and they stripped him and beat him, and went away leaving him half dead. And by coincidence a priest was going down on that road, and when he saw him, he passed by on the other side. Likewise, a Levite also, when he came to the place and saw him, passed by on the other side. But a Samaritan who was on a journey came upon him; and when he saw him, he **felt compassion, and came to him and bandaged up his wounds, pouring oil and wine on them; and he put him on his own animal, and brought him to an inn and took care of him.** On the next day he took out two denarii and gave them to the innkeeper and said, 'Take care of him; and whatever more you spend, when I return, I will repay you.' Which of these three do you think proved to be a neighbor to the man who fell into the robbers' hands?' And he said, 'The one who showed **compassion** to him.' Then Jesus said to him, 'Go and do the same.'" (Luke 10:25-37).

This parable shows how true compassion leads to acts of undeserved grace. Jesus was a man of action during his earthly ministry, vigorously demonstrating both **Compassion** and **Grace** in accord with Isaiah's prophecy:

"The Spirit of the Lord is upon Me,
Because He anointed Me to bring good news to the poor.
He has sent Me to proclaim release to captives,
And recovery of sight to the blind,
To set free those who are oppressed...."
(Isaiah 61:1; Luke 4:18).

THE SERMON ON THE MOUNT

Unquestionably, many of the early Christians connected Jesus's proclamations on the "Mount" to Moses's encounter on Sinai. In a sense, it was a restatement of the heart of the "Law" in "relationship language," delivered by a "second" Moses. Jesus assured the large crowd gathered on the hillside that,

> *"Blessed are the **gentle**, for they will inherit the earth.*
> *Blessed are those who hunger and thirst for righteousness,*
> *for they will be satisfied.*
> *Blessed are the **merciful**, for they will receive **mercy**.*
> *Blessed are the pure in heart, for they will see God.*
> *Blessed are the peacemakers, for they will be called sons of God."*
> (Matthew 5:5-9).

People who are quick to anger are *not* gentle. The "peacemakers" and the "gentle" are those who are **slow to anger**. Jesus used different terms to strike the same points made in God's proclamation on Sinai.

CHESED

Describing the breadth of God's **CHESED**, Jesus said, *"You have heard that it was said, 'You shall love your neighbor and hate your enemy.' But I say to you, love your enemies and pray for those who persecute you, so that you may prove yourselves to be **sons of your Father** Who is in heaven; for He causes His sun to rise on the evil and the good, and sends rain on the righteous and the unrighteous. For if you love those who love you, what reward do you have? Even the tax collectors, do they not do the same? And if you greet only your brothers and sisters, what more are you doing than others? Even the Gentiles, do they not do the same? Therefore, you shall be perfect, as your **heavenly Father** is perfect."* (Matthew 5:43-48).

FORGIVENESS

*"Then it happened that as Jesus was reclining at the table in the house, behold, many tax collectors and sinners came and began dining with Jesus and His disciples. And when the Pharisees saw this, they said to His disciples, 'Why is your Teacher eating with the tax collectors and sinners?' But when Jesus heard this, He said, "It is not those who are healthy who need a physician, but those who are sick. Now go and learn what this means: 'I desire **compassion**, rather than sacrifice,' for I did not come to call the righteous, but sinners."* (Matthew 9:10-13).

Jesus's whole goal is reconciliation. He intentionally went to those who needed forgiveness to the greatest degree and ended up giving his very life so that iniquities, rebellions, and sins might be forgiven. Yes, there are still consequences even where forgiveness is extended. Jesus's death was the most sobering consequence. The New Covenant as understood by Christians does not negate consequences. But God's **CHESED, RACHUWM,** and **CHANNUWN** continue to usher in forgiveness (remember **NOSEI**).

ATTITUDE TOWARD THE *TANAKH*

Because his teachings differentiated between what the common people were seeing displayed in the lives of religious leaders and in the heart of the Commandments, he encouraged them not to

"presume that I came to abolish the Law or the Prophets; I did not come to abolish, but to fulfill. For truly I say to you, until heaven and earth pass away, not the smallest letter or stroke of a letter shall pass from the Law, until all is accomplished! Therefore, whoever nullifies one of the least of these command-ments, and teaches others to do the same, shall be called least in the kingdom of heaven; but whoever keeps and teaches them, he shall be called great in the kingdom of heaven. (Matthew 6:17-19).

APOSTOLIC LETTERS

The Apostle Paul, former Pharisee and student of Rabbi Gamaliel, wrote a short letter to a community of believers in Colossae, a small town about 100 miles east of Ephesus. This letter of instruction was one of the earliest received into the canon of New Testament Scriptures. Paul included almost all of the attitudes and actions recorded in Exodus 34:6-7 in his instructions:

*"So, as those who have been chosen of God, holy and beloved, **put on a heart of compassion, kindness, humility, gentleness and patience; bearing with one another, and forgiving each other, whoever has a complaint against anyone; just as the Lord forgave you, so also should you. Beyond all these things put on love, which is the perfect bond of unity.**"* (Colossians 3:12-14).

The Apostle John, when testifying to the Godly character of Jesus as well as his prophetic mantle, wrote, *"And the Word became flesh, and dwelt among us, and we saw His glory, glory as of the only begotten from the **Father**, full of **GRACE [CHARIS]** and **TRUTH [ALETHEIA]**."* (*The Gospel of John* 1:14). In one sense, for John, Grace and Truth validated Jesus's mission. The Greek **CHARIS** ties us back to **CHESED** as well as **CHANNUWN**, and **ALETHEIA** ties us back to **EMETH**, that is, directly to God's proclamation.

The Apostle Paul, writing to a congregation of early Christians, focused on **CHARIS** (think **CHESED/CHANNUWN**) as the distinctive idea behind Jesus's sacrificial action:

"For you know the GRACE *[CHARIS] of our Lord Jesus Christ, that though He was rich, yet for your sake He became poor, so that you through His poverty might become rich."* (2nd Corinthians 8:9).

About four years later, Paul, on course to Jerusalem for imprisonment and eventual martyrdom in Rome, summed up his personal mission with these words:

*"But I do not consider my life of any account as dear to myself, so that I may finish my course and the ministry which I received from the Lord Jesus, to testify solemnly of the gospel [good news] of the GRACE [**CHARIS**] of God."* (Acts 20:24).

WHO AM I ANYWAY?

For the early Christians, God was the source of Grace, Truth and Steadfast Love. They wanted to walk thoroughly in the ways of God. Today, each one of us, whether Christian or Jew, must answer one essential question. Our answers will frame the picture of who *WE* truly are and whether or not we want to emulate the image of God in our individual lives.

Who *should* we be? In all our thoughts, in the words that we say, in the actions we take, can we reflect the Almighty? Can we move in every relationship with deep compassion, extend generosity and graciousness, exhibit the utmost faithfulness and loyal love, be slow to anger, and be anxious to forgive the worst iniquity? Or, as the Prophet Micah said, can we do justice, be kind, and walk humbly before our God?

Indeed, what does it mean to be a human being? Are we wholly devoted to God or not? May the LORD of the Universe, the great King overall, grant each of us the ability to answer with an authentic and resounding, "YES!"

*"LORD [יְהוָה], God [**ELOHIYM**] of Israel,*
*there is no God [**ELOHIYM**] like You in heaven above or on earth beneath,*
*keeping the covenant [**BERIYTH**] and showing faithfulness [**CHESED**] to*
Your servants who walk before You with all their heart!" (1 Kings 8:23).

GLOSSARY

APAYIM – *anger*

ALAPHIM – *thousands*

AVON – *iniquity (twisted)*

AVOT – *fathers (parents)*

AVRAHAM – *Abraham*

BAMIDBAR – *Book of Numbers*

BANIM – *sons (children)*

BERESHIT – *Book of Genesis*

BERIYTH (BRIT) – *a cutting (covenant)*

BRIT – *cutting (covenant)*

CHANNUWN – *gracious*

CHATTAH'AH – *sin (missing the mark)*

CHESED – *steadfast love*

DEVARIM – *Book of Deuteronomy*

DEVREI HAYAMIM – *Book of Chronicles*

DOWR – *generation(s)*

EL – *God*

ELEPH – *thousand*

ELOHIYM – *God, gods, angels, judges*

EMETH (EMET) – *truth*

EREKH APAYIM – *slow to anger*

HASHEM – *The Name (God)*

KARATH – *cut*

KATHAB – *graven*

LEV – *heart*

MASHIYACH / MASHACH – *Anointed One / anointed*

MELACHIM – *Book of Kings*

MISHLEI – *Book of Proverbs*

MISHNEH – *study*

MITZVOT – *commandment*s

MOSHE – *Moses*

NAQEI – *clearing*

V'NAQEI LO Y'NAQEI – *not clearing*

NASEI – *forgiving*

NOTZER – *keeping*

PAGASH – *meet, join*

PESHA – *rebellion*

POQED – *visit*

QODESH – *Holy*

RACHAM – *have compassion*

RACHUWM – *compassionate*

RAV – *abounding*

RECHEM – *womb*

RIBE'IM – *fourth generation*

SHEMOS – *Book of Exodus*

SHILLESH – *third generation*

SHMUEL – *Samuel*

TANAKH – *Hebrew Bible*

TEHILLIM – *Book of Psalms*

TESHUVAH – *repentance*

TORAH – *Teachings (Law)*

V'AL-BANEI VANIM – *sons of sons (grandchildren)*

YAAKOV – *Jacob*

YAHWEH (YA-hei-VAH) – *I was, I am, I always will be*[37]

YESHAYAH – *Isaiah*

YIRMIYAH – *Jeremiah*

YITZHAK – *Isaac*

---

37   *("I am now what I always was and always will be,"* Maimonides. God's Memorial Name)

APPENDIX A
SHORT-HAND LEXICON

What follows is a short-hand lexicon of a portion of Exodus 34:6-7 in transliterated Hebrew—a combination that borrows from multiple sources including *Strong's Concordance* and a modified *King James Lexicon*. First come the full Hebrew verses from the Leningrad Codex, then each Hebrew word is taken separately in order (from right to left). Below that is how the Hebrew sounds could be written in bold English letters. Then, the directly related translation from the *New English Translation of the Book of Exodus, Vol. 2*, as published in 1997 and edited by Rabbi A.J. Rosenberg is in bold. Finally, a short definition in italics. I have rearranged the *New English Translation* to better conform to the Hebrew word order.

וַיַּעֲבֹ֨ר יְהֹוָ֥ה ׀ עַל־פָּנָיו֮ וַיִּקְרָא֒

יְהֹוָ֣ה ׀ יְהֹוָ֔ה אֵ֥ל רַח֖וּם וְחַנּ֑וּן אֶ֥רֶךְ אַפַּ֖יִם וְרַב־חֶ֥סֶד
וֶאֱמֶֽת׃

נֹצֵ֤ר חֶ֙סֶד֙ לָאֲלָפִ֔ים נֹשֵׂ֥א עָוֺ֛ן וָפֶ֖שַׁע וְחַטָּאָ֑ה וְנַקֵּה֙ לֹ֣א
יְנַקֶּ֔ה פֹּקֵ֣ד ׀ עֲוֺ֣ן אָב֗וֹת עַל־בָּנִים֙ וְעַל־בְּנֵ֣י בָנִ֔ים עַל־
שִׁלֵּשִׁ֖ים וְעַל־רִבֵּעִֽים׃

וַיַּעֲבֹר

Va-ya'avor (Ya'avor)

Passed before

*to cross over; used very widely of any transition (literal or
figurative; transitive, intransitive, intensive, causative);
specifically, to cover (in copulation).*

יְהוָה

YHVH (YHWH, Yahweh, Yhovah)

the LORD

*(the) Self-Existent or Eternal; (the) One Who Is;
God's Memorial Name revealed to Moses at the Burning Bush;
HASHEM (the Name); the LORD.*

עַל־פָּנָיו

al-panav (al-paniym)

him

*the face (as the part that turns); used in a great variety of
applications (literally and figuratively); also (with prepositional prefix)
as a preposition (before, etc.).*

וַיִּקְרָא

va-yikra

and proclaimed

*to call out to (i.e., properly, address by name, but used in
a wide variety of applications).*

אֵל

EL

God

strength; as adjective, mighty; especially the Almighty
(but used also of any deity).

רַחוּם

rachuwm (rachum, rahum)

Who is compassionate

Deeply compassionate—full of compassion, like a mother for her child.

וְחַנּוּן

v'channuwn (v'hannun)

and gracious

gracious—generous—full of mercy—graceful.

אֶרֶךְ

erech (arek)

slow

Long, long-suffering, long-winged, patient, slow.

אַפַּיִם

apayim

to anger

the nose or nostril; hence, the face, and occasionally a person;
also (from the rapid breathing in passion) ire, anger.

וְרַב
v'rav (rav)
and abundant
abundant (in quantity, size, age, number, rank, quality).

וֶאֱמֶת
v'emeth (v'emet)
and truth
stability, (figuratively) certainty, truth, as things really are, trustworthiness, assuredness, firmness, established, faithful, right, sure, true.

נֹצֵר
notser (natsar)
preserving
to guard, in a good sense to protect, maintain, obey, or in a bad sense to conceal.

חֶסֶד
chesed (hesed, khesed, chessed, checed)
in loving-kindness
loyal, kind, steadfast, loving, faithful (to promises), solid; by implication (towards God) piety; rarely (by opposition) reproof; beauty.

לָאֲלָפִים
la'alaphim
for thousands
hence (the ox's head being the first letter of the alphabet, this eventually used as a numeral) a thousand thousand.

נֹשֵׂא

nosei (nasa, nose)

forgiving

to lift or carry, bear away; in a great variety
of applications, literal and figurative.

עָוֹן

avon

iniquity

perversity, iniquity, twistedness, bentness, mischief, intentional sin.

וָפֶשַׁע

and rebellion

va-pesha (va-phesha, va-fesha)

beyond the boundaries, beyond authority, rebellion,
intentional sin, transgression, trespass.

וְחַטָּאָה

v'chatta'ah (chatta'ah, v'hata-a)

and sin

miss the mark, an offence (sometimes habitual sinfulness), and its penalty,
occasion, sacrifice, or expiation; also (concretely) an offender.

וְנַקֵּה

v'naqei (naqah, v'nakeh)

to be (or make) clean; by implication (in an adverse sense) root out.

לֹא

lo

yet He does not completely

not, no, none, nay, never, neither, ere, otherwise, before.

יְנַקֶּה

y'naqei (naqah, y'nakeh)

clear [of sin]

to be (or make) clean, pure; hold innocent, acquit;
by implication (in an adverse sense) root out.

פֹּקֵד

poqed (paqad)

He visits

to visit (with friendly or hostile intent); by analogy, to oversee,
muster, charge, care for, miss, deposit, etc.

אָבוֹת

avot

of parents

fathers, in a literal and immediate, or figurative and remote application)—
chief, (fore-)father(-less), patrimony, principal.

עַל־בָּנִים

al-banim

on the children

son(s)—as a builder of the family name; in the widest sense
(of literal and figurative) relationship, including grandson,
subject, nation, quality or condition, etc.

וְעַל־בְּנֵי

v'al-banei

and the children's

*son(s)—as a builder of the family name; in the widest sense
(of literal and figurative) relationship, including grandsons,
subject, nation, quality or condition, etc.*

בָּנִים

vanim

children

sons, children.

עַל־שִׁלֵּשִׁים

al-shilleshim

to the third

*descendants of the third degree, that is,
great grandchildren—third (generation).*

וְעַל־רִבֵּעִים

v'al-ribe'im

and fourth generations

*unto descendants of the fourth generation—
the great great grandchildren—fourth.*

APPENDIX B

TRANSLATIONS OF EXODUS 34:6-7

American Standard Version

(ASV) And Jehovah passed by before him, and proclaimed, Jehovah, Jehovah, a God merciful and gracious, slow to anger, and abundant in loving-kindness and truth, keeping loving-kindness for thousands, forgiving iniquity and transgression and sin, and that will be no means clear the guilty, visiting the iniquity of the fathers upon the children, and upon the children's children, upon the third and upon the fourth generation.

Christian Standard Bible (Holman)

(CSB) Then the Lord passed in front of him and proclaimed: Yahweh-Yahweh is a compassionate and gracious God, slow to anger and rich in faithful love and truth, maintaining faithful love to a thousand generations, forgiving wrongdoing, rebellion, and sin. But He will not leave the guilty unpunished, bringing the consequences of the fathers' wrongdoing on the children and grandchildren to the third and fourth generation.

Complete Jewish Bible

(CJB) ADONAI passed before him and proclaimed: "YUD-HEH-VAV-HEH!!! Yud-Heh-Vav-Heh [ADONAI] is God, merciful and compassionate, slow to anger, rich in grace and truth; showing grace to the thousandth generation, forgiving offenses, crimes and sins; yet not exonerating the guilty, but causing the negative effects of the parents' offenses to be experienced by their children and grandchildren, and even by the third and fourth generations."

---

38   Versions generally taken from biblehub.org, biblegateway.com and blueletterbible.com

Coverdale (1535)

And whan ye LORDE passed by before his face, he cryed: LORDE LORDE, God, mercifull & gracious, & longe sufferinge, and of greate mercy and trueth, thou that kepest mercy in stoare for thousandes, and forgeuest wickednes, trespace and synne (before whom there is no man innocent) thou that visitest the wickednesse of the fathers vpon ye children and childers children, vnto the thirde and fourth generacion.

Darby Translation

(DBY) And Jehovah passed by before his face, and proclaimed, Jehovah, Jehovah God merciful and gracious, slow to anger, and abundant in goodness and truth, keeping mercy unto thousands, forgiving iniquity and transgression and sin, but by no means clearing the guilty; visiting the iniquity of the fathers upon the children, and upon the children's children, upon the third and upon the fourth generation.

Douay-Rheims 1899 Catholic Bible

(RHE) And when he passed before him, he said: O the Lord, the Lord God, merciful and gracious, patient and of much compassion, and true, Who keepest mercy unto thousands: Who takest away iniquity, and wickedness, and sin, and no man of himself is innocent before thee. Who renderest the iniquity of the fathers to the children, and to the grandchildren, unto the third and fourth generation.

English Standard Version

(ESV) The LORD passed before him and proclaimed, "The LORD, the LORD, a God merciful and gracious, slow to anger, and abounding in steadfast love and faithfulness, keeping steadfast love for thousands, forgiving iniquity and transgression and sin, but Who will by no means clear the guilty, visiting the iniquity of the fathers on the children and the children's children, to the third and the fourth generation."

Geneva Bible (1599)

(GNV) So the Lord passed before his face, and [a]cried, The Lord, the Lord, strong, merciful, and gracious, slow to anger, and abundant in goodness and truth. Reserving mercy for thousands, forgiving iniquity, and transgression and sin, and not making the *wicked* innocent, visiting the iniquity of the fathers upon the children, and upon children's children, unto the third and fourth *generation.*

Good News Translation

(GNT) The Lord then passed in front of him and called out, "I, the Lord, am a God Who is full of compassion and pity, Who is not easily angered and Who shows great love and faithfulness. I keep my promise for thousands of generations and forgive evil and sin; but I will not fail to punish children and grandchildren to the third and fourth generation for the sins of their parents."

Hebrew Names Version

(HNV) The LORD passed by before him, and proclaimed, "The LORD! the LORD, a merciful and gracious God, slow to anger, and abundant in loving-kindness and truth, keeping loving-kindness for thousands, forgiving iniquity and disobedience and sin; and that will by no means clear the guilty, visiting the iniquity of the fathers on the children, and on the children's children, on the third and on the fourth generation."

Israel Bible

Hashem passed before him and proclaimed: "*Hashem! Hashem!* a *Hashem* compassionate and gracious, slow to anger, abounding in kindness and faithfulness, extending kindness to the thousandth generation, forgiving iniquity, transgression, and sin; yet He does not remit all punishment, but visits the iniquity of parents upon children and children's children, upon the third and fourth generations."

Jewish Publication Society (*Tanakh* 1917)

(JPS 1917) And the LORD passed by before him, and proclaimed: "The LORD, the LORD, God, merciful and gracious, long-suffering, and abundant in goodness and truth; keeping mercy unto the thousandth generation, forgiving iniquity and transgression and sin; and that will by no means clear the guilty; visiting the iniquity of the fathers upon the children, and upon the children's children, unto the third and unto the fourth generation."

Jewish Publication Society (*Tanakh* 1985)

(NJPS) The Lord passed before him and proclaimed: "The LORD! The LORD!, a God compassionate and gracious, slow to anger, abounding in kindness and faithfulness, Extending kindness to the thousandth generation, forgiving iniquity, transgression and sin; yet He does not remit all punishment, but visits the iniquity of parents upon children and children's children, upon the third and fourth generations."

Jubilee Bible 2000

(JUB) And as the LORD passed by before him, he proclaimed, I AM, I AM strong, merciful, and gracious, long-suffering, and abundant in mercy and truth, keeping mercy for thousands, letting go of iniquity and rebellion and sin; and by no means will I absolve the guilty, visiting the iniquity of the fathers upon the sons and upon the sons' sons, unto the third and to the fourth *generation.*

King James Version

(KJV) And the LORD passed by before him, and proclaimed, The LORD, The LORD God, merciful and gracious, long-suffering, and abundant in goodness and truth, Keeping mercy for thousands, forgiving iniquity and transgression and sin, and that will by no means clear the guilty; visiting the iniquity of the fathers upon the children, and upon the children's children, unto the third and to the fourth generation.

La Sainte Bible, Louis Segond 1910

Et l'Éternel passa devant lui, et s'écria: L'Éternel, l'Éternel, Dieu miséri-
cordieux et compatissant, lent à la colère, riche en bonté et en fidélité, qui
conserve son amour jusqu'à mille générations, qui pardonne l'iniquité, la
rébellion et le péché, mais qui ne tient point le coupable pour innocent, et
qui punit l'iniquité des pères sur les enfants et sur les enfants des enfants
jusqu'à la troisième et à la quatrième génération!

La Sainte Bible, Segond, 2ⁿᵈ Rev. 1978

Et l'Éternel passa devant lui, et s'écria: L'Éternel, l'Éternel, Dieu compatissant et qui fait grâce, lent à la colère, riche en bienveillance et en fidélité,
qui conserve sa bienveillance jusqu'à mille generations, qui pardonne la
faute, le crime et le péché, mais qui ne tient pas (le coupable) pour innocent, et qui punit la faute des pères sur les fils et sur les petits fils jusqu'à la
troisième et à la quatrième génération!

Lexham English Bible

(LEB) And Yahweh passed over before him, and he proclaimed, "Yahweh,
Yahweh, God, *Who is* compassionate and gracious, *slow to anger*, and
abounding with loyal love and faithfulness, keeping loyal love to the thousands, forgiving iniquity and transgression and sin, and he does not leave
utterly unpunished, punishing the guilt of fathers on sons and on sons of
sons on third and fourth *generations.*"

New American Bible (Revised)

(NAB) So the Lord passed before him and proclaimed: The Lord, the Lord,
a God gracious and merciful, slow to anger and abounding in love and
fidelity, continuing his love for a thousand generations, and forgiving wickedness, rebellion, and sin; yet not declaring the guilty guiltless, but bringing punishment for their parents' wickedness on children and children's
children to the third and fourth generation!

New American Standard Bible (1995)

(NASB) Then the LORD passed by in front of him and proclaimed, "The LORD, the LORD God, compassionate and gracious, slow to anger, and abounding in loving-kindness and truth; Who keeps loving-kindness for thousands, Who forgives iniquity, transgression and sin; yet He will by no means leave the guilty unpunished, visiting the iniquity of fathers on the children and on the grandchildren to the third and fourth generations."

New Century Version

(NCV) The Lord passed in front of Moses and said, "I am the Lord. The Lord is a God Who shows mercy, Who is kind, Who doesn't become angry quickly, Who has great love and faithfulness, and is kind to thousands of people. The Lord forgives people for evil, for sin, and for turning against him, but he does not forget to punish guilty people. He will punish not only the guilty people, but also their children, their grandchildren, their great-grandchildren, and their great-great-grandchildren."

New English Translation (Judaica Press) edited by A. J. Rosenberg

And the LORD passed before him and proclaimed: "יְהֹוָה יְהֹוָה, God, Who is compassionate and gracious, slow to anger, and abundant in loving-kindness and truth; preserving loving-kindness for thousands, forgiving iniquity, rebellion and sin; yet He does not completely clear [of sin]. He visits the iniquity of parents on the children and the children's children to the third and fourth generations."

New International Version

(NIV) And he passed in front of Moses, proclaiming, "The LORD, the LORD, the compassionate and gracious God, slow to anger, abounding in love and faithfulness, maintaining love to thousands, and forgiving wickedness, rebellion and sin. Yet he does not leave the guilty unpunished; he punishes the children and their children for the sin of the parents to the third and fourth generation."

New King James Version

(NKJV) And the Lord passed before him and proclaimed, "The Lord, the Lord God, merciful and gracious, longsuffering, and abounding in goodness and truth, keeping mercy for thousands, forgiving iniquity and transgression and sin, by no means clearing *the guilty*, visiting the iniquity of the fathers upon the children and the children's children to the third and the fourth generation."

New Living Translation translated by Rabbi A. Kaplan

(NLT) The LORD passed in front of Moses, calling out, "Yahweh! The LORD! The God of compassion and mercy! I am slow to anger and filled with unfailing love and faithfulness. I lavish unfailing love to a thousand generations. I forgive iniquity, rebellion, and sin. But I do not excuse the guilty. I lay the sins of the parents upon their children and grandchildren; the entire family is affected—even children in the third and fourth generations."

New Revised Standard Version

(NRSV) The LORD passed before him, and proclaimed, "The LORD, the LORD, a God merciful and gracious, slow to anger, and abounding in steadfast love and faithfulness, keeping steadfast love for the thousandth generation, forgiving iniquity and transgression and sin, yet by no means clearing the guilty, but visiting the iniquity of the parents upon the children and the children's children, to the third and the fourth generation."

Orthodox Jewish Bible

(OJB) And Hashem passed by before him, and proclaimed, Hashem, Hashem El Rachum v'Channun, slow to anger, and abundant in chesed and emes, Preserving chesed for thousands, forgiving avon and pesha and chatta'ah, and by no means leaving the guilty unpunished; visiting the avon of the avot upon the banim, and upon the bnei banim, unto the third and to the fourth generation.

Revised Standard Version

(RSV) The LORD passed before him, and proclaimed, "The LORD, the LORD, a God merciful and gracious, slow to anger, and abounding in steadfast love and faithfulness, keeping steadfast love for thousands, forgiving iniquity and transgression and sin, but Who will by no means clear the guilty, visiting the iniquity of the fathers upon the children and the children's children, to the third and the fourth generation."

Septuagint LLX

(LLX) καὶ παρῆλθεν κύριος πρὸ προσώπου αὐτοῦ καὶ ἐκάλεσεν κύριος ὁ θεὸς οἰκτίρμων καὶ ἐλεήμων μακρόθυμος καὶ πολυέλεος καὶ ἀληθινὸς καὶ δικαιοσύνην διατηρῶν καὶ ποιῶν ἔλεος εἰς χιλιάδας ἀφαιρῶν ἀνομίας καὶ ἀδικίας καὶ ἁμαρτίας καὶ οὐ καθαριεῖ τὸν ἔνοχον ἐπάγων ἀνομίας πατέρων ἐπὶ τέκνα καὶ ἐπὶ τέκνα τέκνων ἐπὶ τρίτην καὶ τετάρτην γενεάν

The Living Torah

God passed by before [Moses] and proclaimed, God, God, Omnipotent, merciful and kind, slow to anger, with tremendous [resources of] love and truth. He remembers deeds of love for thousands [of generations], forgiving sin, rebellion, and error. He does not clear [those who do not repent] but keeps in mind the sins of the fathers to their children and grandchildren, to the third and fourth generation.

The Jerusalem Bible

(TJB) Yahweh passed before him and proclaimed, "Yahweh, Yahweh, a God of tenderness and compassion, slow to anger, rich in kindness and faithfulness; for thousands he maintains his kindness, forgives faults, transgression, sin; yet he lets nothing go unchecked, punishing the father's fault in the sons and in the grandsons to the third and fourth generation."

The Message Bible

(MSG) God passed in front of him and called out, "God, God, a God of mercy and grace, endlessly patient—so much love, so deeply true—loyal in love for a thousand generations, forgiving iniquity, rebellion, and sin. Still, he doesn't ignore sin. He holds sons and grandsons responsible for a father's sins to the third and even fourth generation."

The Webster Bible

(WBT) And the LORD passed by before him, and proclaimed, The LORD, The LORD God, merciful and gracious, long-suffering, and abundant in goodness and truth. Keeping mercy for thousands, forgiving iniquity and transgression and sin, and that will by no means clear the guilty; visiting the iniquity of the fathers upon the children, and upon the children's children, to the third and to the fourth generation.

Vulgate

quo transeunte coram eo ait Dominator Domine Deus misericors et clemens patiens et multae miserationis ac verus qui custodis misericordiam in milia qui aufers iniquitatem et scelera atque peccata nullusque apud te per se innocens est qui reddis iniquitatem patrum in filiis ac nepotibus in tertiam et quartam progeniem.

Wycliffe 1382

(WYC) and when the Lord passed before him (yea, when the Lord passed before him), he said, Lordshipper, Lord God, merciful, and pious, patient, and of much mercy doing, and soothfast, which keepest covenant and mercy into thousands, which doest away wickedness, and trespasses, and sins, and no man by himself is innocent with thee, which yieldest the wickedness of fathers to their sons, and to the sons of their sons, into the third and the fourth generation. (Who keepest covenant and mercy with thousands *of people*, Who doest away wickedness, and trespasses, and sins, but no one in themselves is innocent with me, and Who punishest their sons, and the sons of their sons, to the third and fourth generations, for the wickedness of their fathers).

Young's Literal Translation
(YLT) and Jehovah passeth over before his face, and calleth: "Jehovah, Jehovah God, merciful and gracious, slow to anger, and abundant in kindness and truth, keeping kindness for thousands, taking away iniquity, and transgression, and sin, and not entirely acquitting, charging iniquity of fathers on children, and on children's children, on a third generation, and on a fourth."

BIBLIOGRAPHY

Bowe, Barbara. *Biblical Foundations of Spirituality*, Lanham, Rowman & Littlefield, 2017, Print.

Brown, F., Driver, S., Bridges, C. *The Brown-Drover-Briggs Hebrew and English Lexicon*, Peabody, Mass., Hendrickson Publishing. 2020, Print.

Irenaeus. *Irenaeus on the Christian Faith*, condensed by James R. Payton, Jr., Cambridge, James Clark & Co., 2012, Print.

Irenaeus. *The Ante-Nicene Fathers, Vol. 1, Against Heresies*, translated by Roberts and Rambaut, Buffalo, The Christian Literature Company, 1885, Print

Kugel, James. *The Great Shift*, Boston, Houghton Mifflin Harcourt, 2017, Print.

Lewis, C. S. *Out of the Silent Planet*, New York, Scribner, Print.

Moses. *The Book of Exodus, Vol. 1 & 2*, edited by Rabbi Roseberg, New York, Judaica Press, 1997, Print.

Moses. *The Living Torah*, translated by Rabbi Aryeh Kaplan, Jerusalem, Maznaum Publishing Corp, 1981, Print.

Maimonides, Moses. *A Maimonides Reader*, edited by Isadore Twersky, Springfield, Behrman, 1972, Kindle.

Maimonides, Moses. *The Guide for the Perplexed*, translated by M. Friedlander, Ph.D, Dover Publications, New York, 1956, Print.

Maimonides, Moses. *Rambam*, Mishne Torah, Yad Hachzakah, annotated & translated by A. Finkel, Scranton, Yeshivah Beth Moshe, 2001, Print.

Moses. *The Book of Exodus*, Vol. 1 & 2, edited by Rabbi Rosenberg, New York, Judaica Press, 1997, Print.

Rashi. *Commentary on Jeremiah*, translated by Freedman, England, Soncino Press, Print.

Schaeffer, Francis. *He is There and He Is Not Silent*, Wheaten, Tyndale, 1972, Print.

Segond, Louis. *La Sainte Bible*, as translated, Amazon, 1910, Kindle.

Snaith, Norman. *The Distinctive Ideas of the Old Testament*, New York, Schocken Books, 1975, Print.

The Holy Scriptures, translated by Eminent Committee of Jewish Scholars, Philadelphia, Jewish Publication Society, 1955, Print.

The Jerusalem Bible, London, Darton, Longman & Todd, 1966, Print.

Trumbull, Clay. *The Blood Covenant*, Kirkwood, MO., Impact Books, 1893, Print.

Theological Dictionary of the Old Testament, Vol I & V, edited by Botterweck & Ringren, translated by D. Green, Grand Rapids, Eerdmans, 1986, Print.

INDEX

A

Aaron xv, 9, 58, 59, 82, 104
Abraham xiii, 6, 9, 21, 23, 25, 26, 43, 59, 61, 62, 84, 103, 104, 105
Abram 61
Absalom 87
Adam and Eve 25, 104
ADONAI 22, 101, 129
Agabus 107
Against Heresies 83, 139
AGAPE 29, 67
ALAPHIM 77, 119
ALETHEIA 117
anger 9, 10, 34, 35, 47, 48, 49, 50, 51, 52, 53, 54, 82, 94, 115, 123
Anna 107
APAYIM 34, 48, 49, 50, 53
Aramaic 108, 113
Ark of the Covenant 20, 60
attributes xv, 13, 15, 26, 53, 68, 100, 106
AVON 34, 81, 82, 84, 85, 86, 88, 89, 92, 93, 95, 96, 97, 119
AVOT 33, 93, 95, 96, 119

B

BAMIDBAR 119
BANIM 93, 95, 97, 119
Barron 51
Bart 94, 95, 96
Bathsheba 84, 90
bent 84, 85, 86, 88, 91
bentness 85, 97, 125
BERESHIT 119
BERIYTH xiii, 59, 60, 62, 63, 64, 108, 118, 119
Bhagavad Gita xii
Bienveillance 69
Bill 43
bitterness 52, 53
Blood Covenant 140
Botterweck 24, 68, 140
Bowe 18, 139
BRIT xiii, 60, 119
Brit bein HaBetarim 59, 62
Brit Hadasha 59

perversity 84, 125
PESHA 81, 82, 84, 86, 87, 88, 89, 92, 120
Peter 107
Pharisees 116
PHILEO 67
Pope 80
POQED 93, 95, 96, 120
Priest 108
Priesthood 59
proclamation 16, 24, 26, 40, 53, 58, 60, 68, 72, 81, 102, 103, 104, 113, 115, 117
Prophet 19, 53, 59, 104, 108, 111, 118
Prophets 2, 89, 103, 104, 107, 108, 116
Proverbs 49, 58, 65, 73, 119
Psalm xiv, 29, 34, 35, 36, 37, 41, 49, 53, 57, 63, 67, 72, 73, 84, 92, 102

Q

QODESH 20, 21, 40, 51, 85, 89, 92, 100, 107, 108, 120

R

RACHAM 28, 31, 33, 34, 41, 53, 54, 63, 67, 84, 120
RACHUWM 27, 28, 29, 30, 31, 33, 34, 35, 36, 37, 39, 40, 41, 45, 47, 49, 55, 71,
72, 83, 84, 100, 108, 116, 120
Ransom 85
Rashi 25, 62, 139
RAV 34, 35, 55, 56, 71, 72, 84, 101, 120
REAL 75
Rebekah 23, 104
rebellion 5, 9, 13, 14, 16, 50, 58, 81, 86, 94, 100, 102, 109, 120, 125, 129, 132, 133,
134, 135, 136, 137
REBELLION 81, 86
RECHEM 27, 120
reconciliation 58, 116
repentance 91, 101, 120
Ringgren 24, 68
Robin Hood 88, 89
Rosenberg 5, 13, 24, 36, 46, 68, 86, 121, 134, 139
RUACH 101, 107
Russell 26, 30
Ruth 66

S

Sachs 89
Sacks 60, 100, 101, 108
salt 64, 65